Published by
Revolutionary Hearts Industries
Illustrated by Naomi Winston

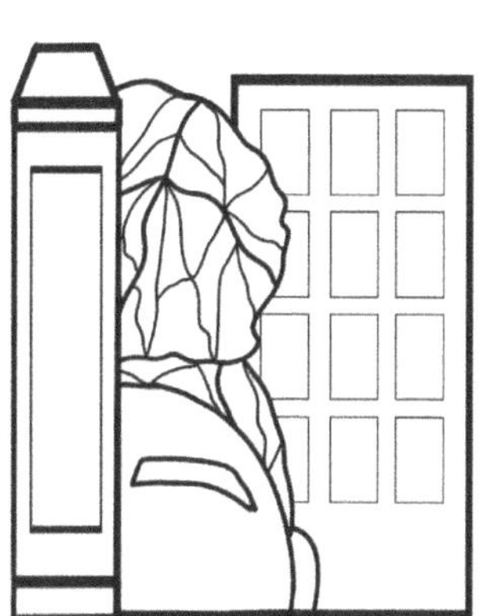

Dear Black Boy,

I tried my best to write this book for you. I cannot relate to you as I can with Black women because I am not a Black man. I will say this:

I have seen you wander through the valley. I have seen you wipe away tears from your face that have never fallen.
I have seen you pick yourself off of the ground with heavy burdens on your back.
I have seen you smile through the tears that you have not let yourself cry. I have seen you shy away from pink in favor of black in fear of being judged.

I have seen your legs grow weary from carrying a heavy soul.
I have seen your eyelids droop as you imagine the bliss of sleep because life has become too hard.
I have seen you become a brother, father, and husband to so many people.

I have seen you become the change that you wish to see.
I have seen your aspirations and your dreams come to life.
I have seen you evolve and wake in the day a new person.

Black boy I may not be able to feel your pain all the way just like you may never be able to see mine. I just want you to know Black boy that I see. I see you for who you are, who you want to be, and where you want to be. You are bigger than your pain, your past, and your fears. You are bigger than all of that.
Cry your tears and let them run down your face like rivers.

Remember, that everything has a purpose and you are everything.

LETTER FROM THE AUTHOR

BLACK MEN ARE THE FUTURE

Words You May Need to Hear:

My heart is open to loving you. You are so important and valuable. You are worth everything the world has to offer and your existence is not dependent on your ability to give. You as an individual person deserve respect, love, and patience. Do not be fearful of what you cannot change in love, in life, or in yourself. Work continuously to be better men and raise better men. Love yourself, the women in your life, and the world you live in enough to want to become a more loving, caring, compassionate, vulnerable, and strong person.

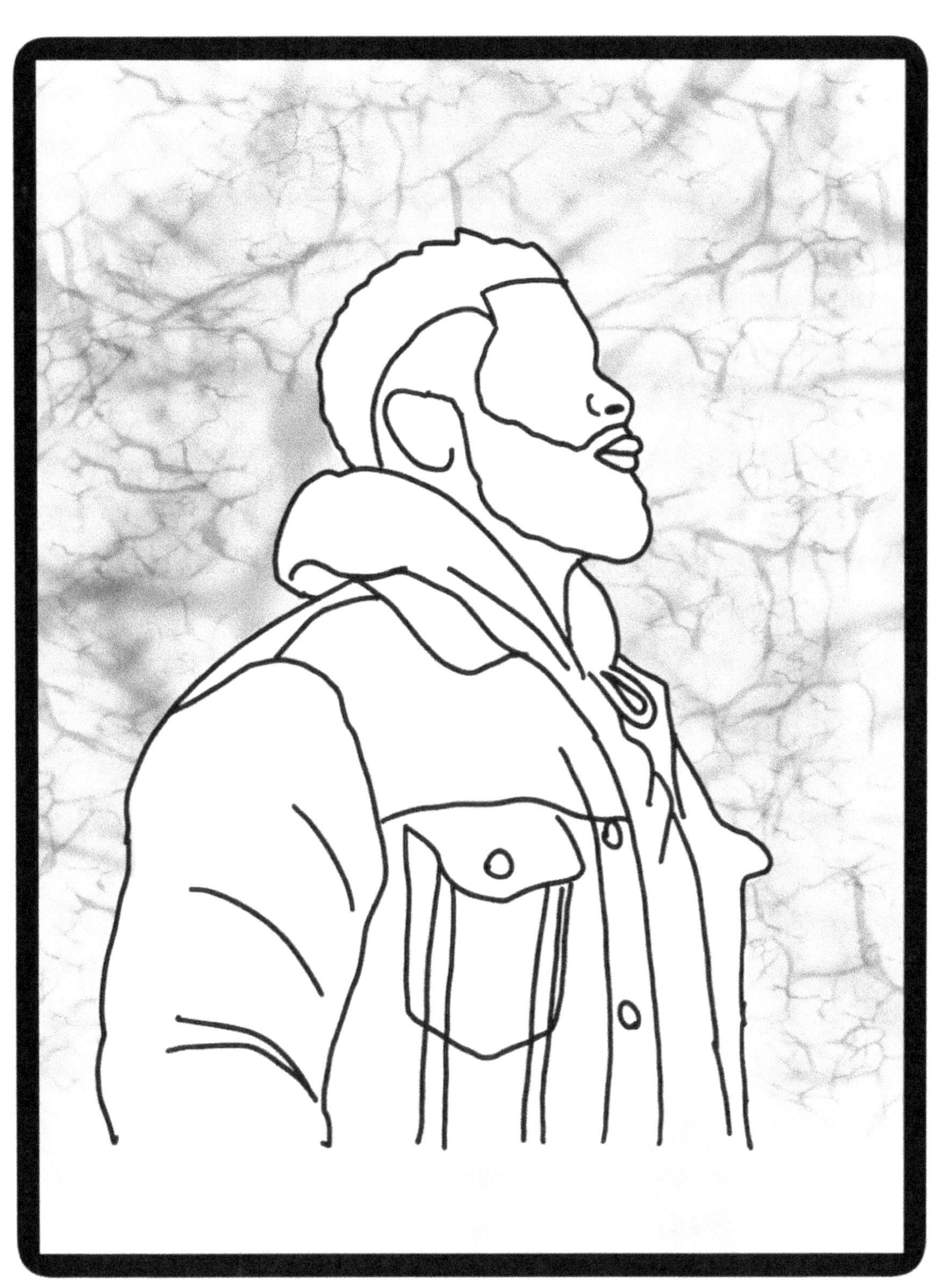

You are feared because they know your power so do not underestimate yourself.

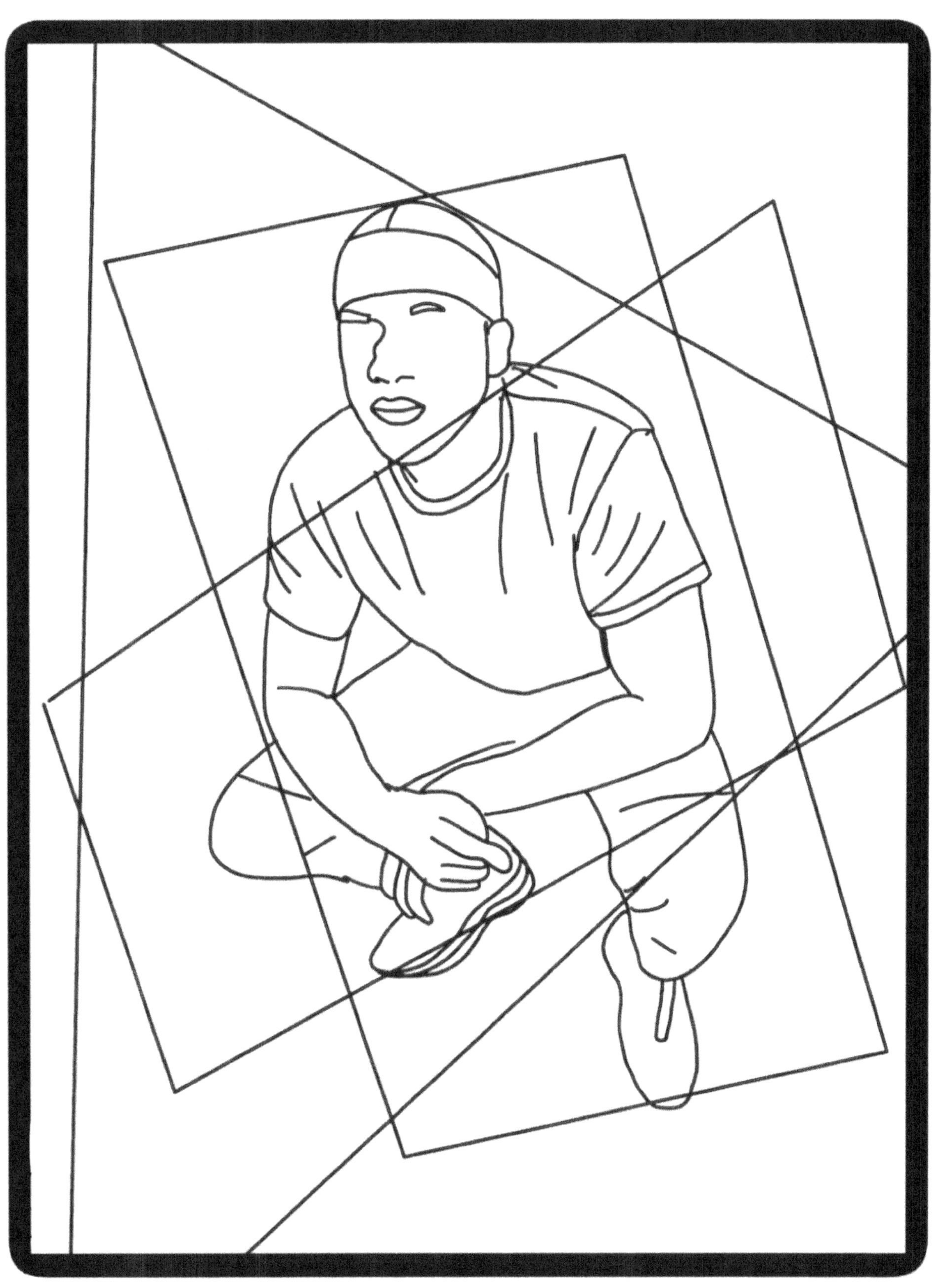

Even when the world is against you
remember that you are not alone.

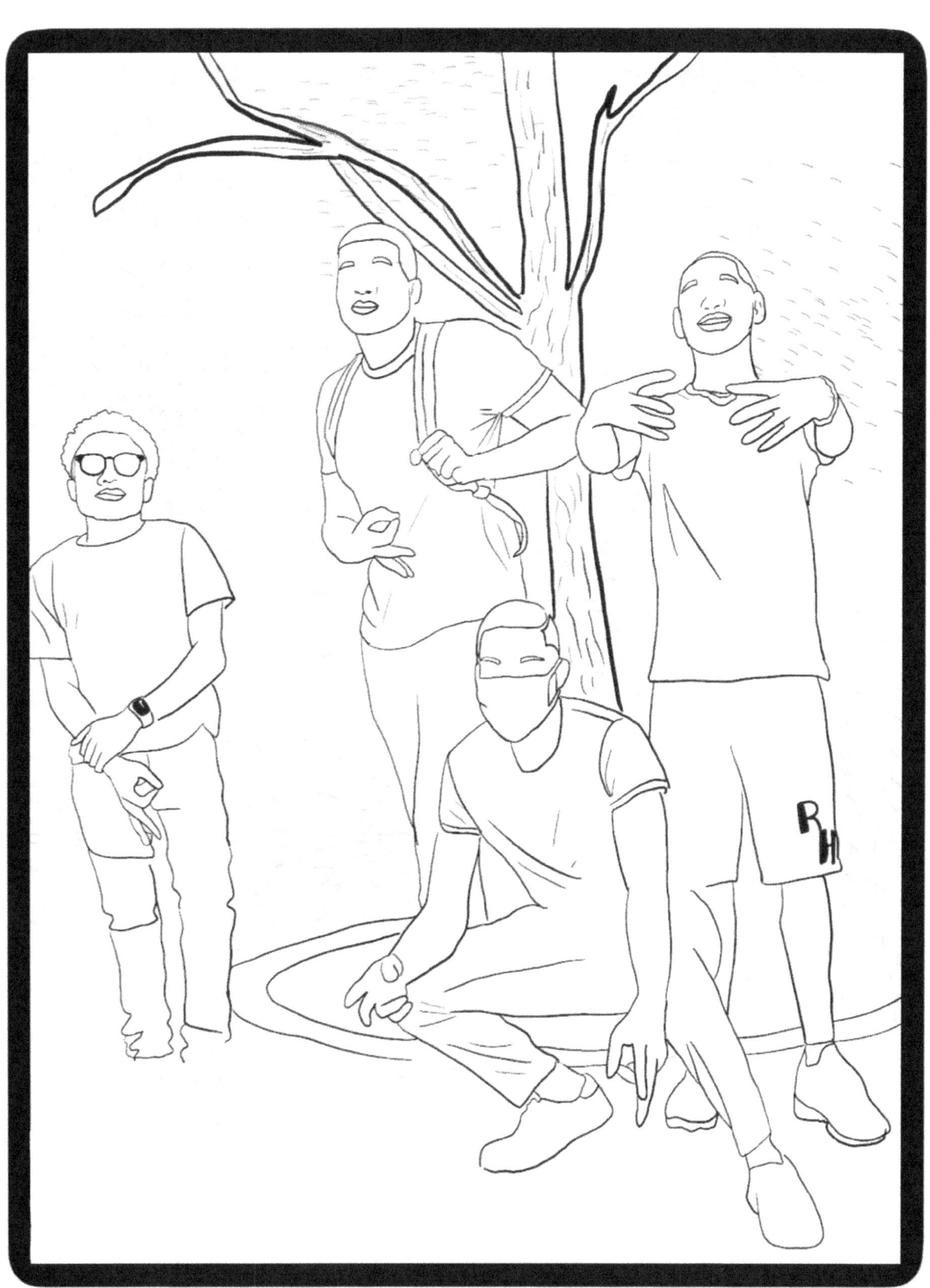

You are loved.

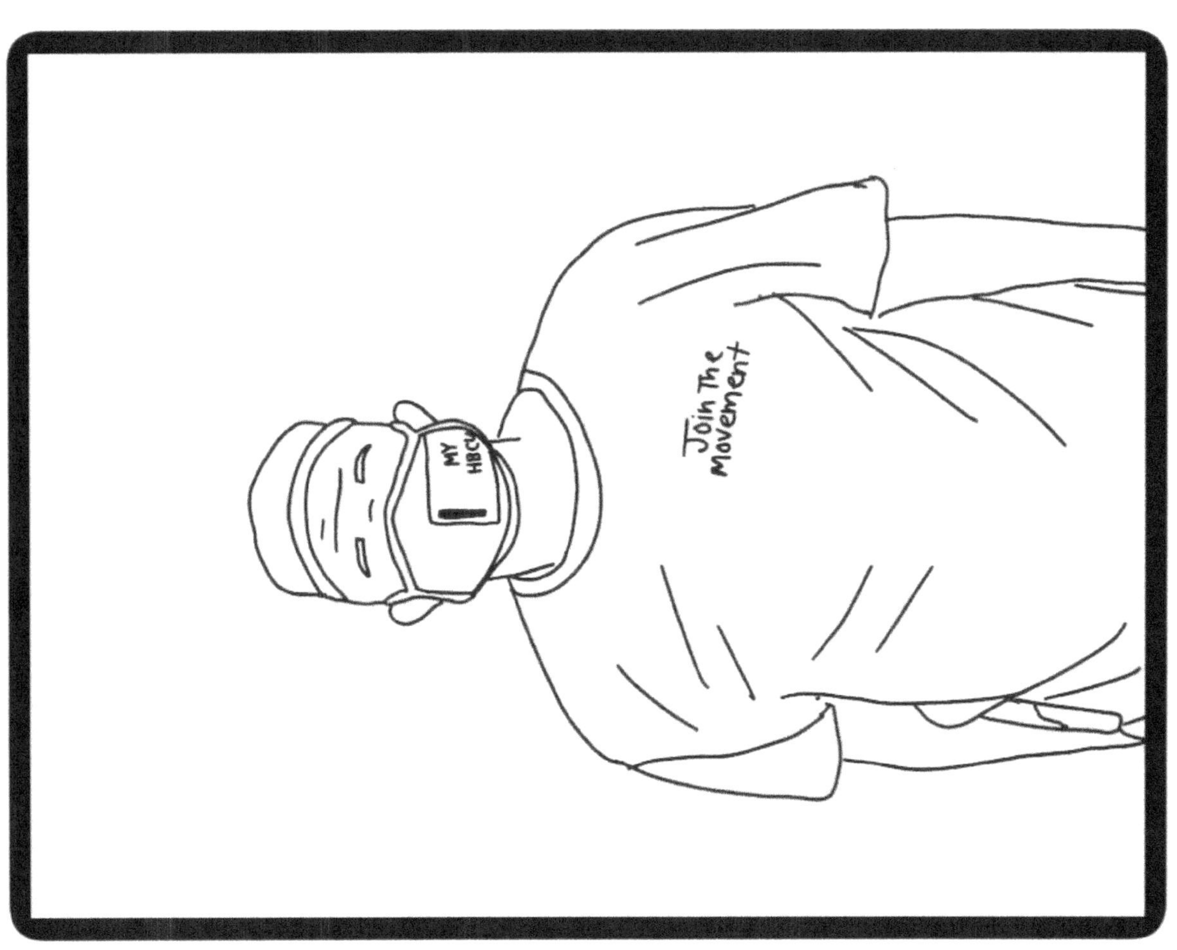

MY HBCU
Join The Movement

You are smart.

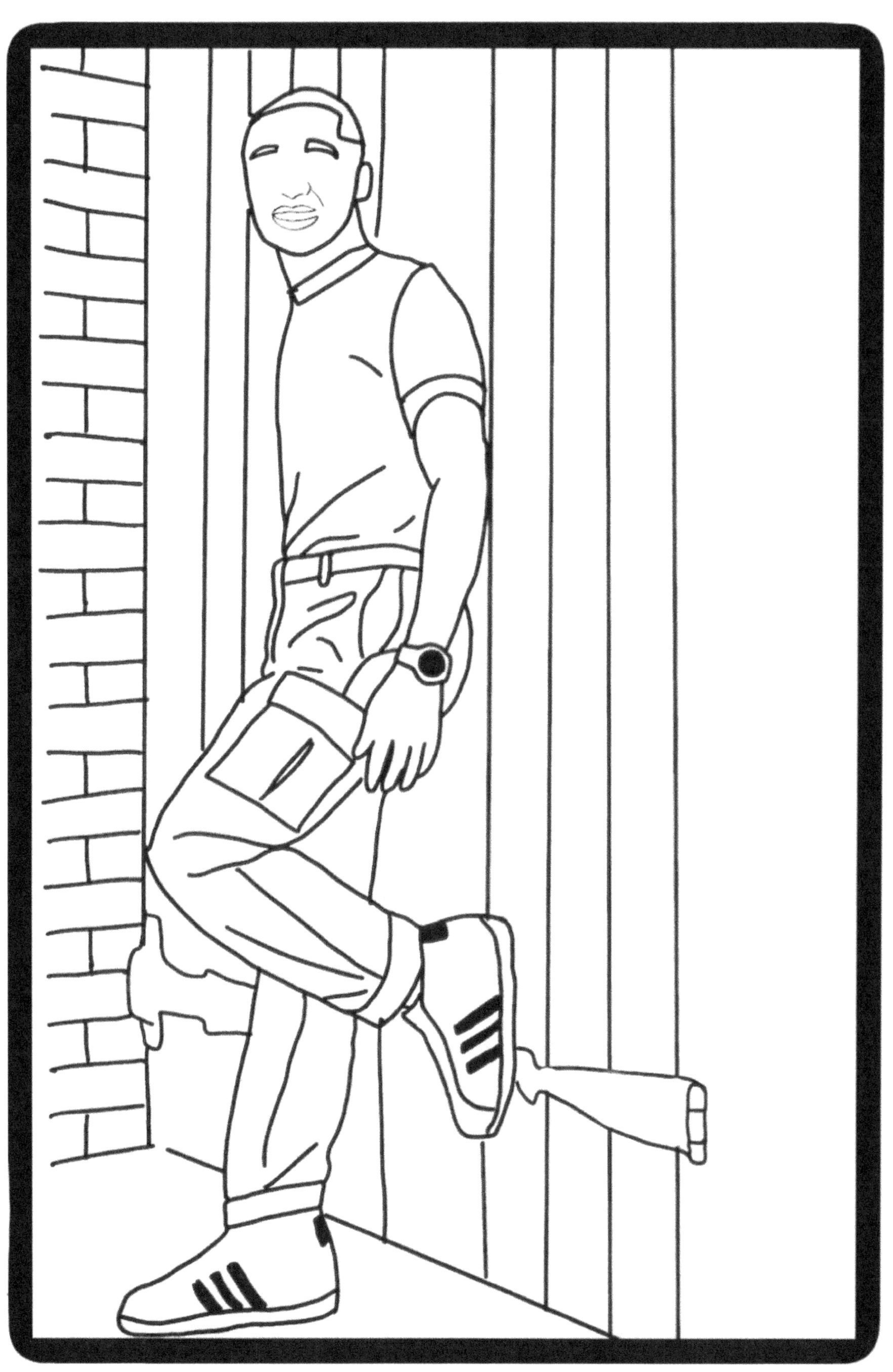

You are valuable.

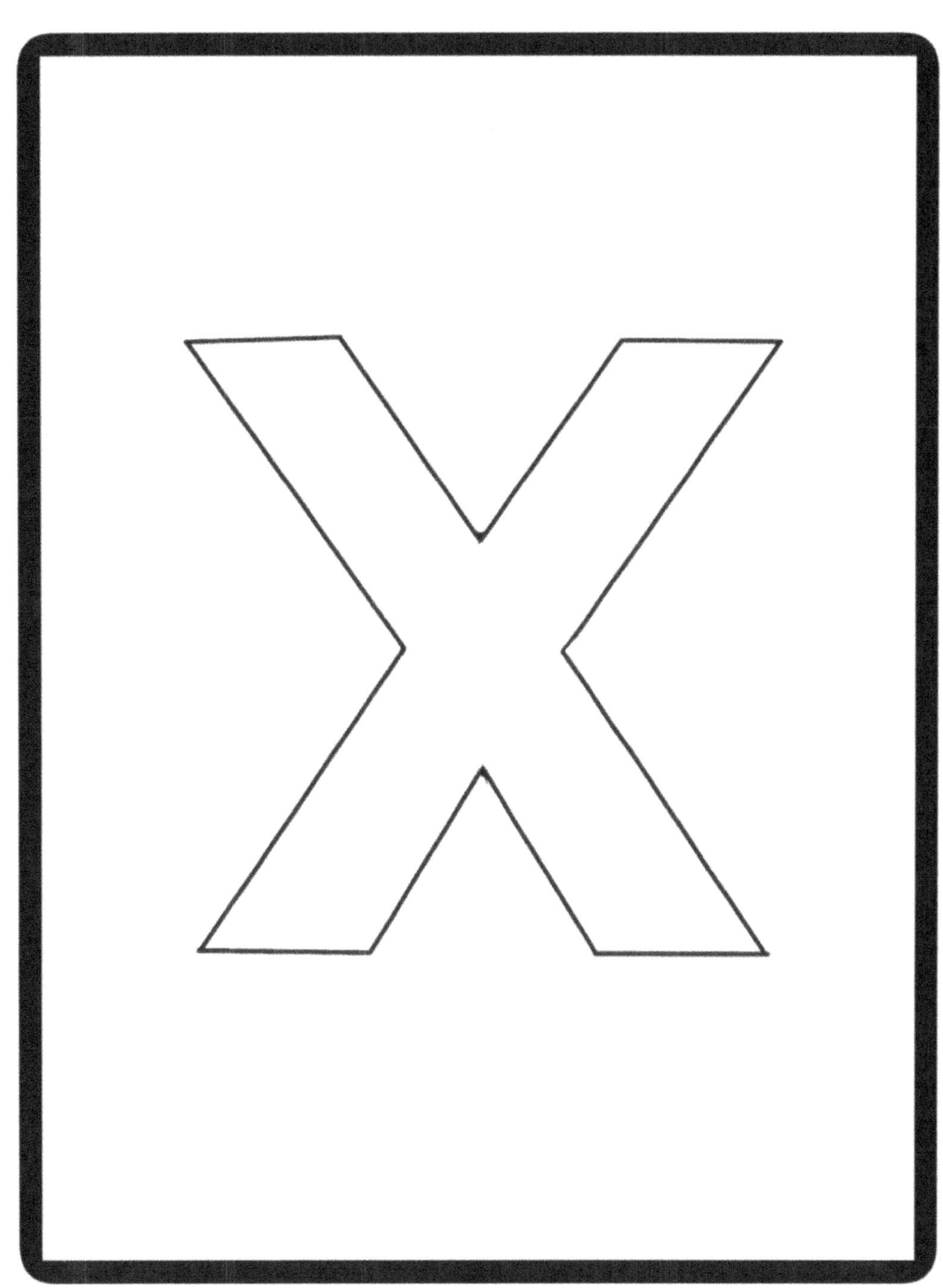

You are gorgeous.

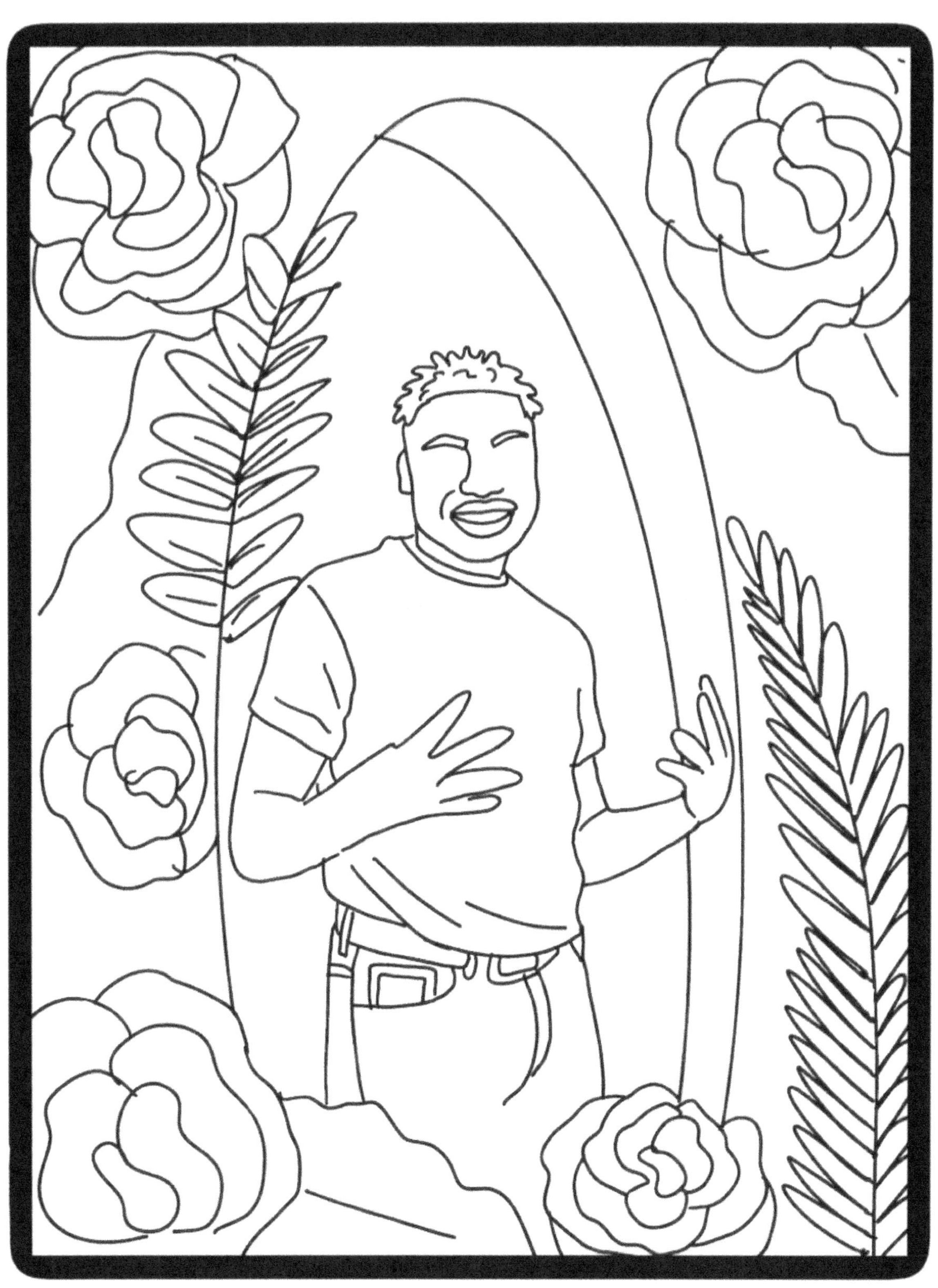

You are not a stereotype.

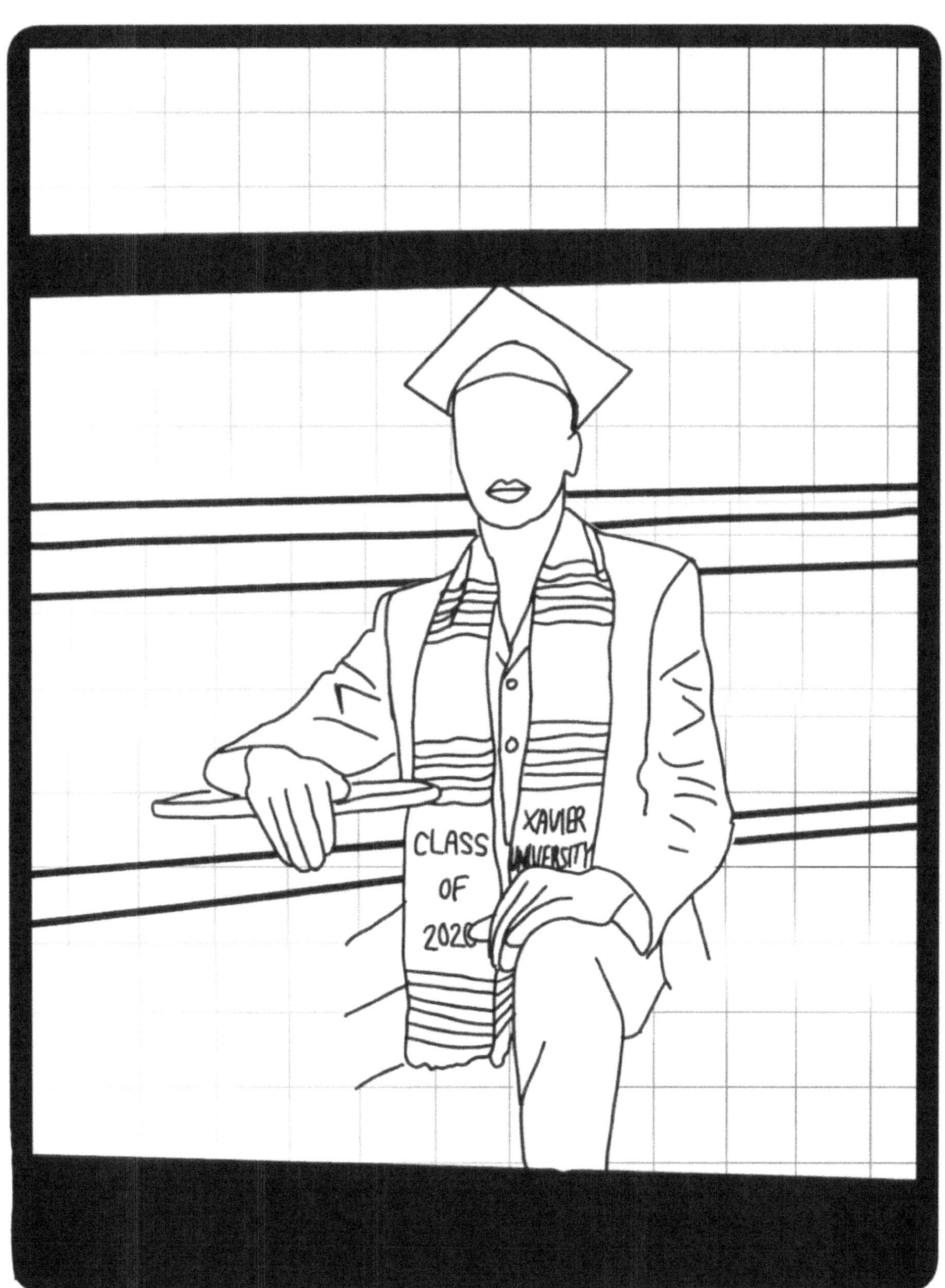

CLASS
OF
2020
XAVIER
UNIVERSITY

There is nothing wrong with letting
yourself rest

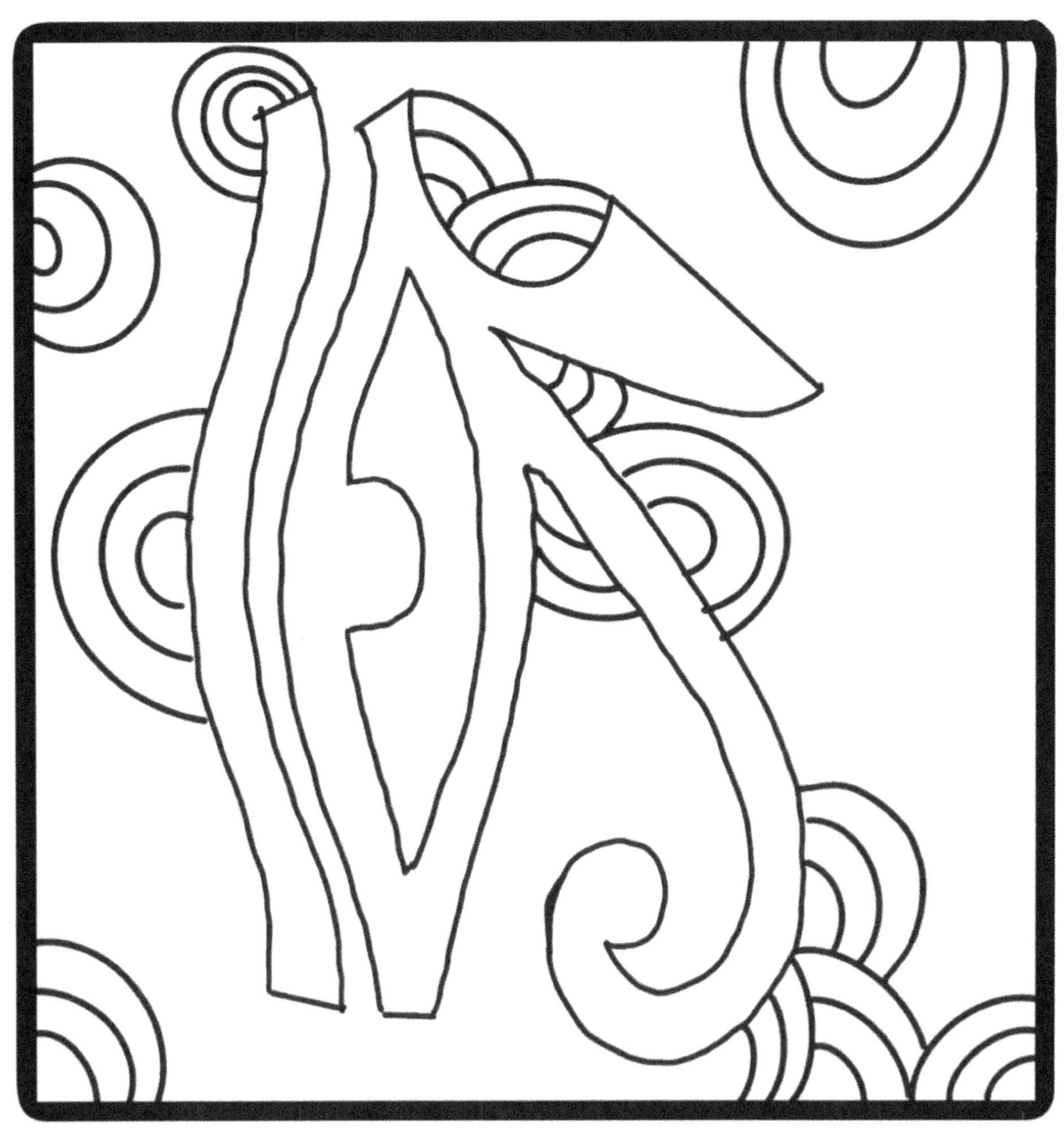

You deserve to be vulnerable.

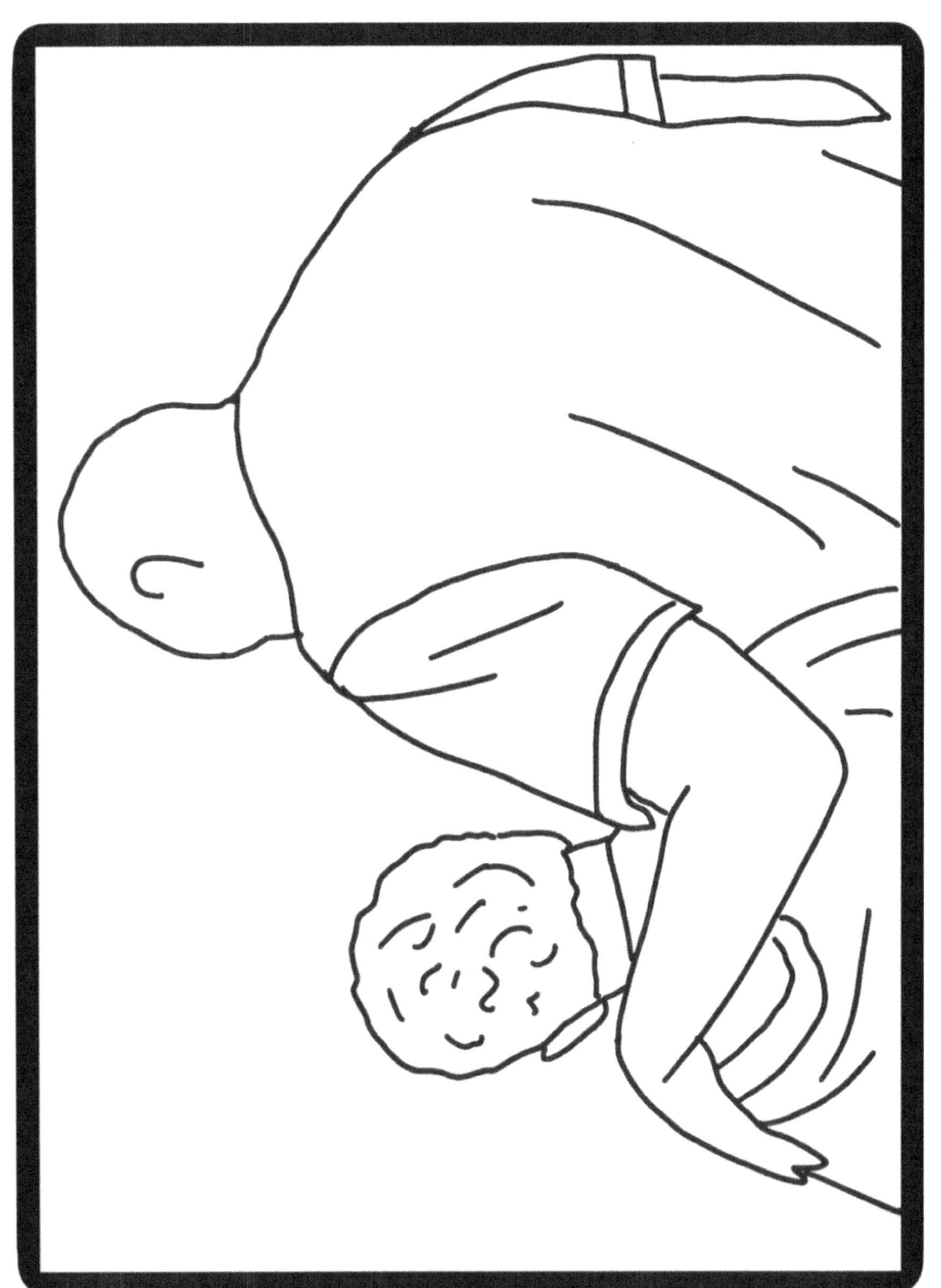

Crying does not make you weak.

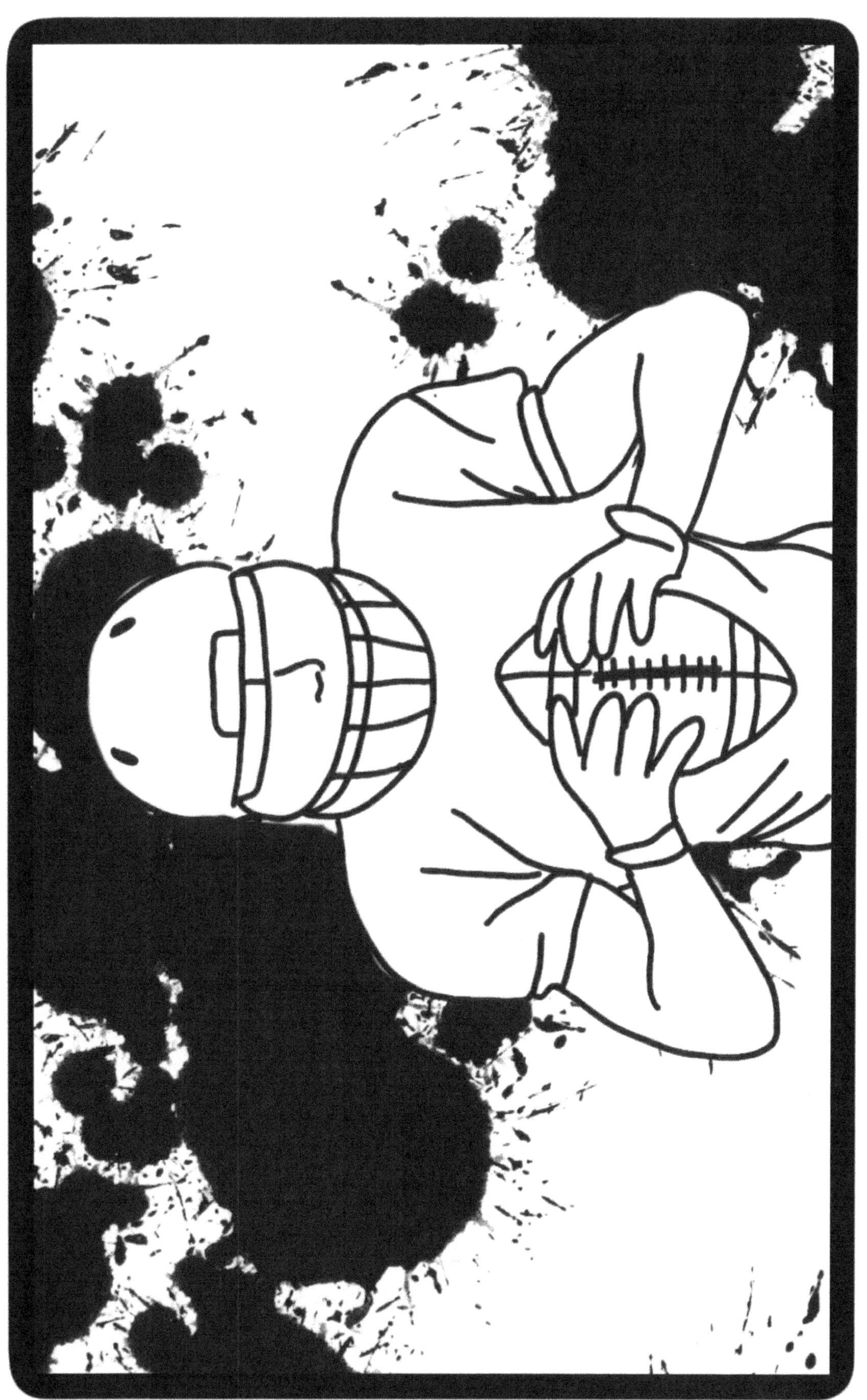

You deserve to be loved.

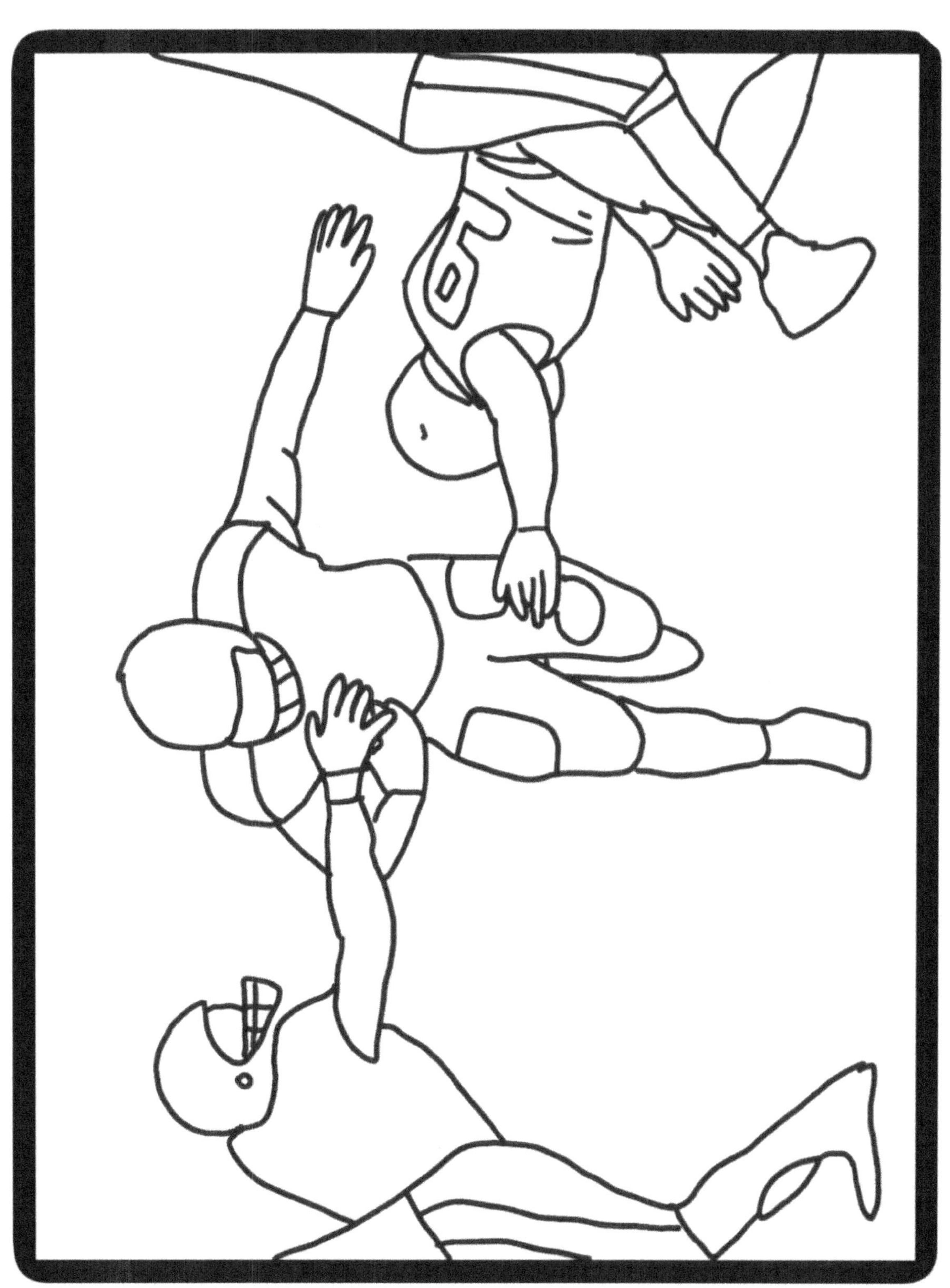

You are valuable.

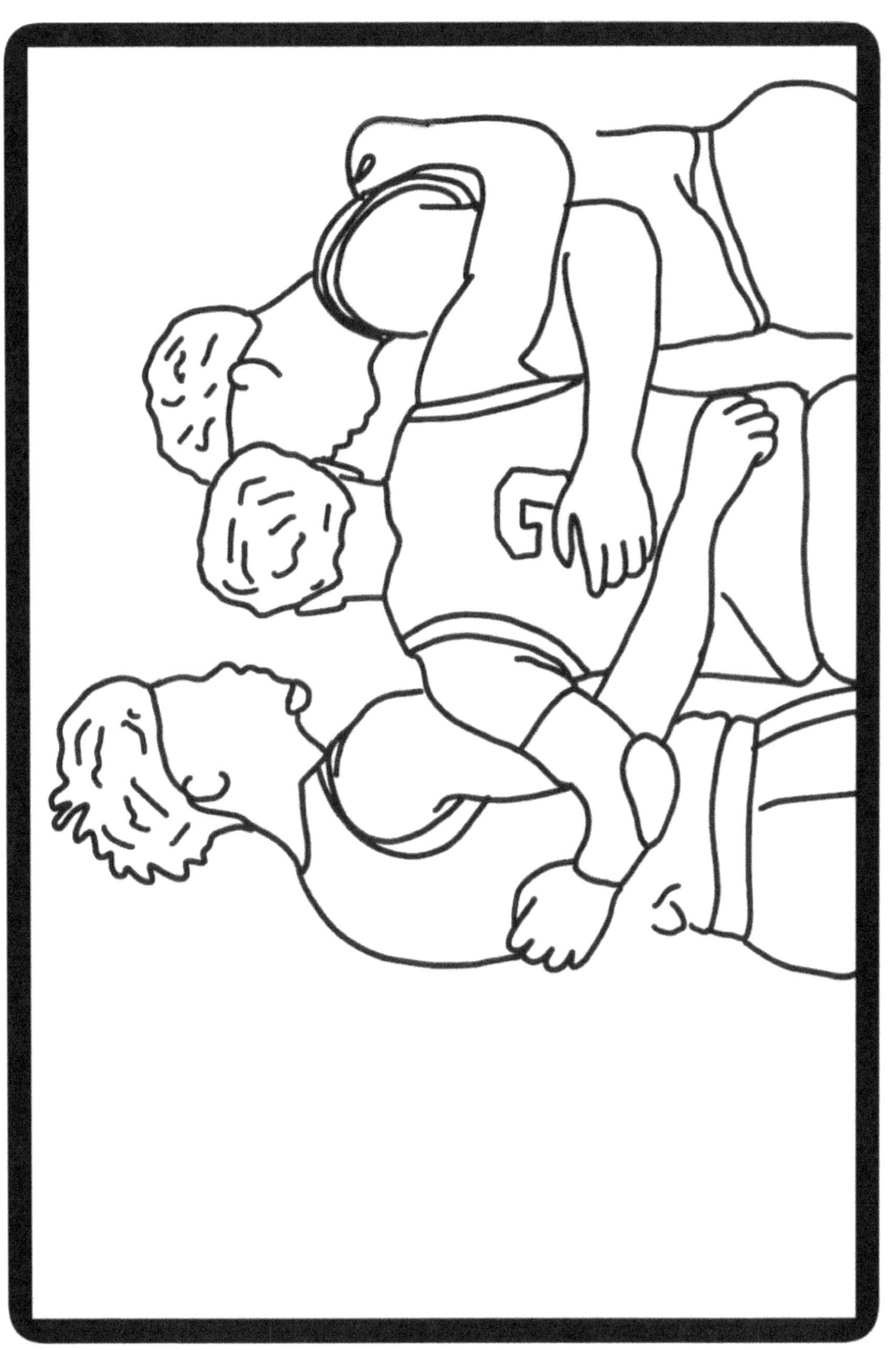

It takes a real man to be able to be himself

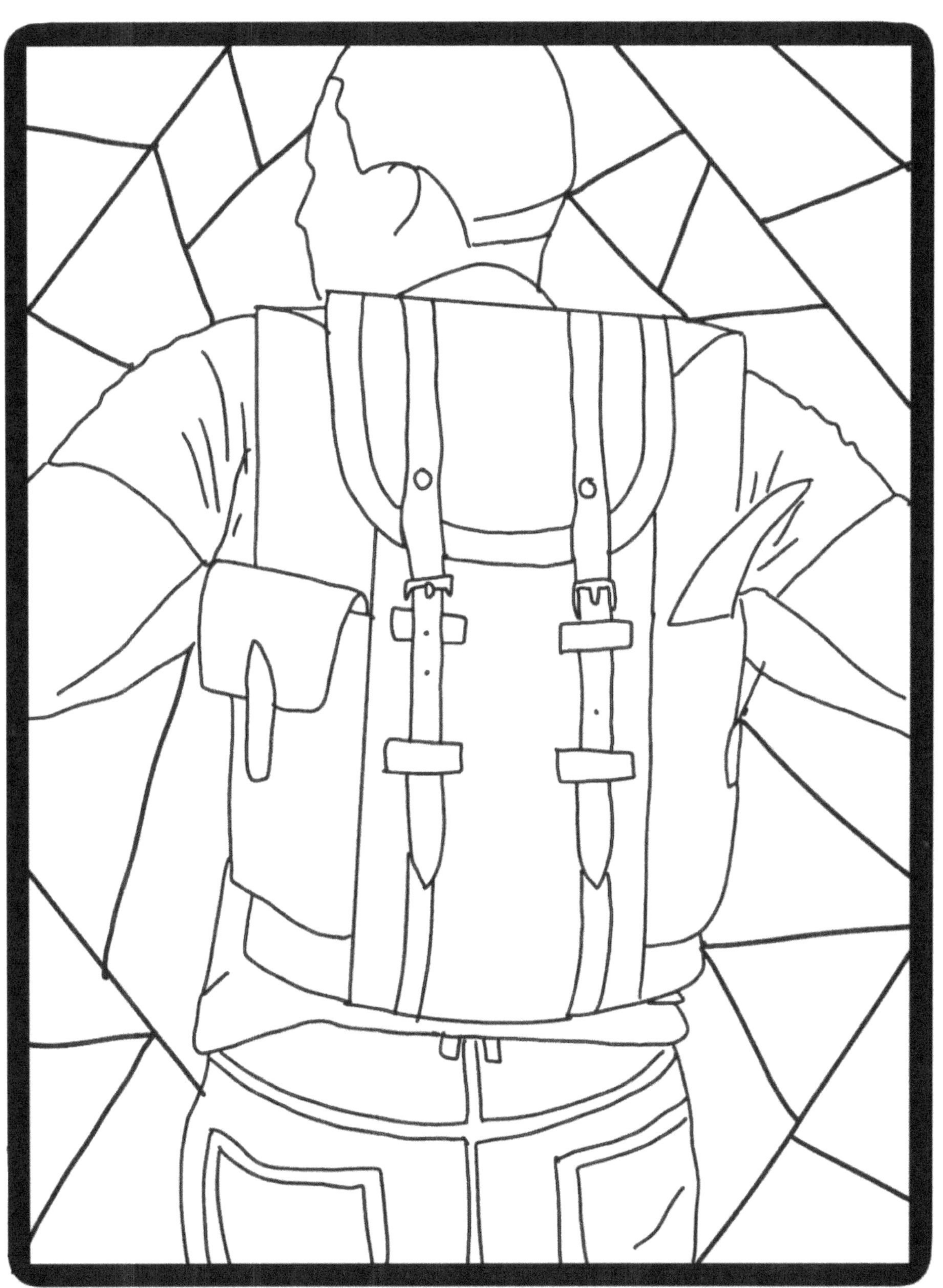

You are important.

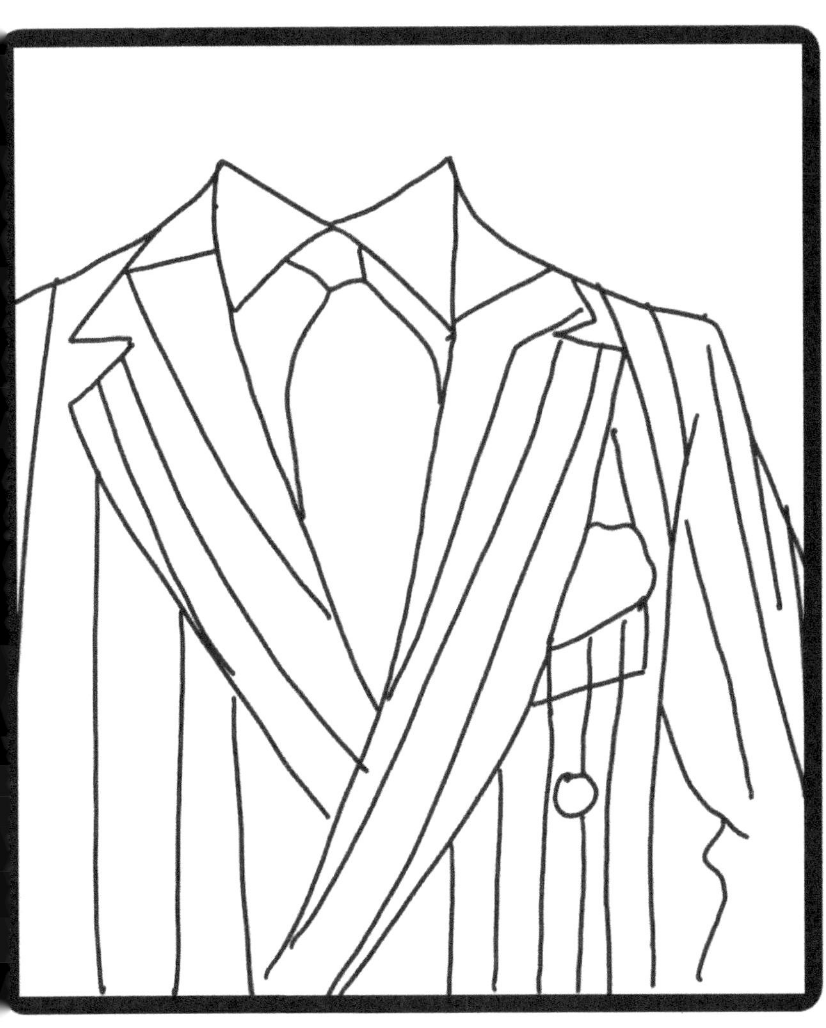

You are not the leaders of tomorrow…where you stand right now is your domain and you are the leader.

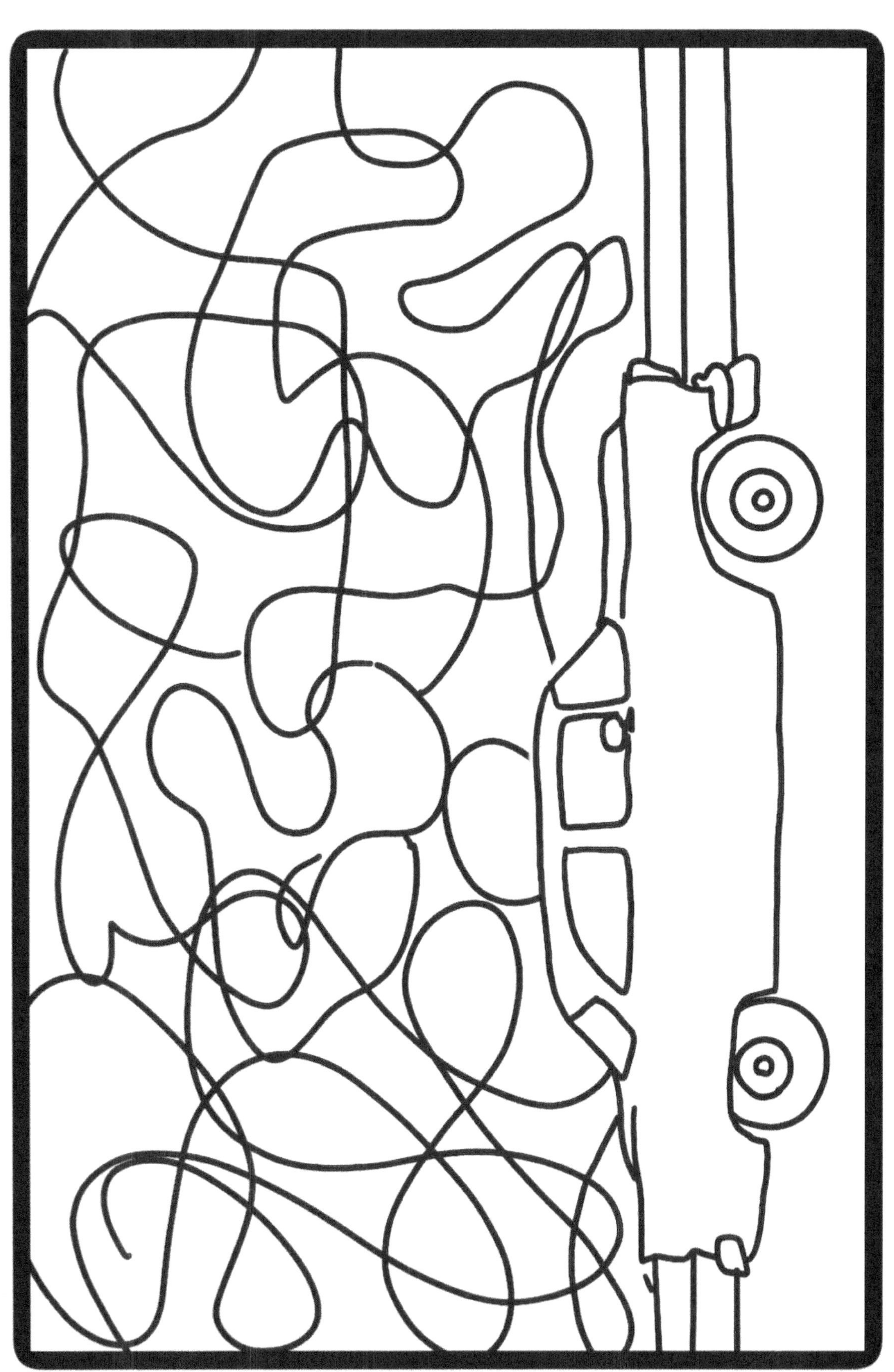

Being feminine doesn't make you less
of a man.

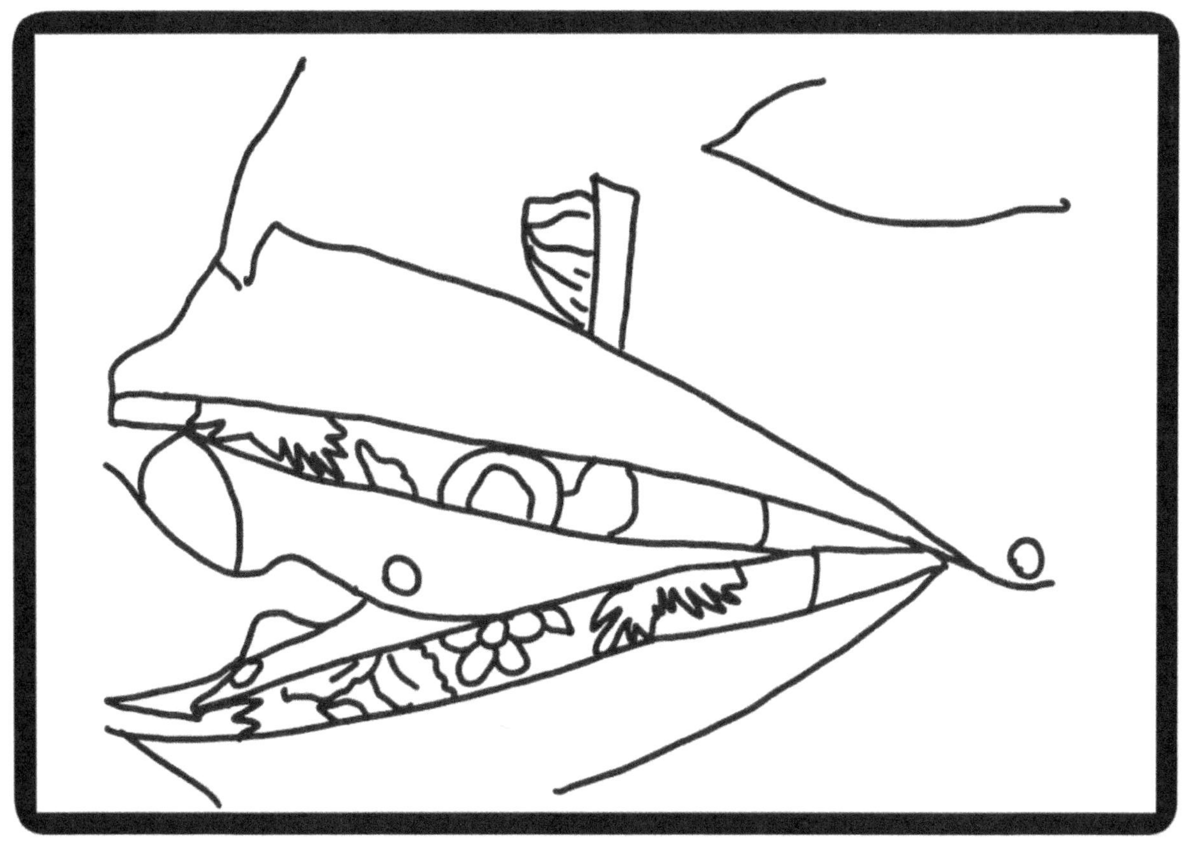

Feelings are not for the weak but
rather for the strong.

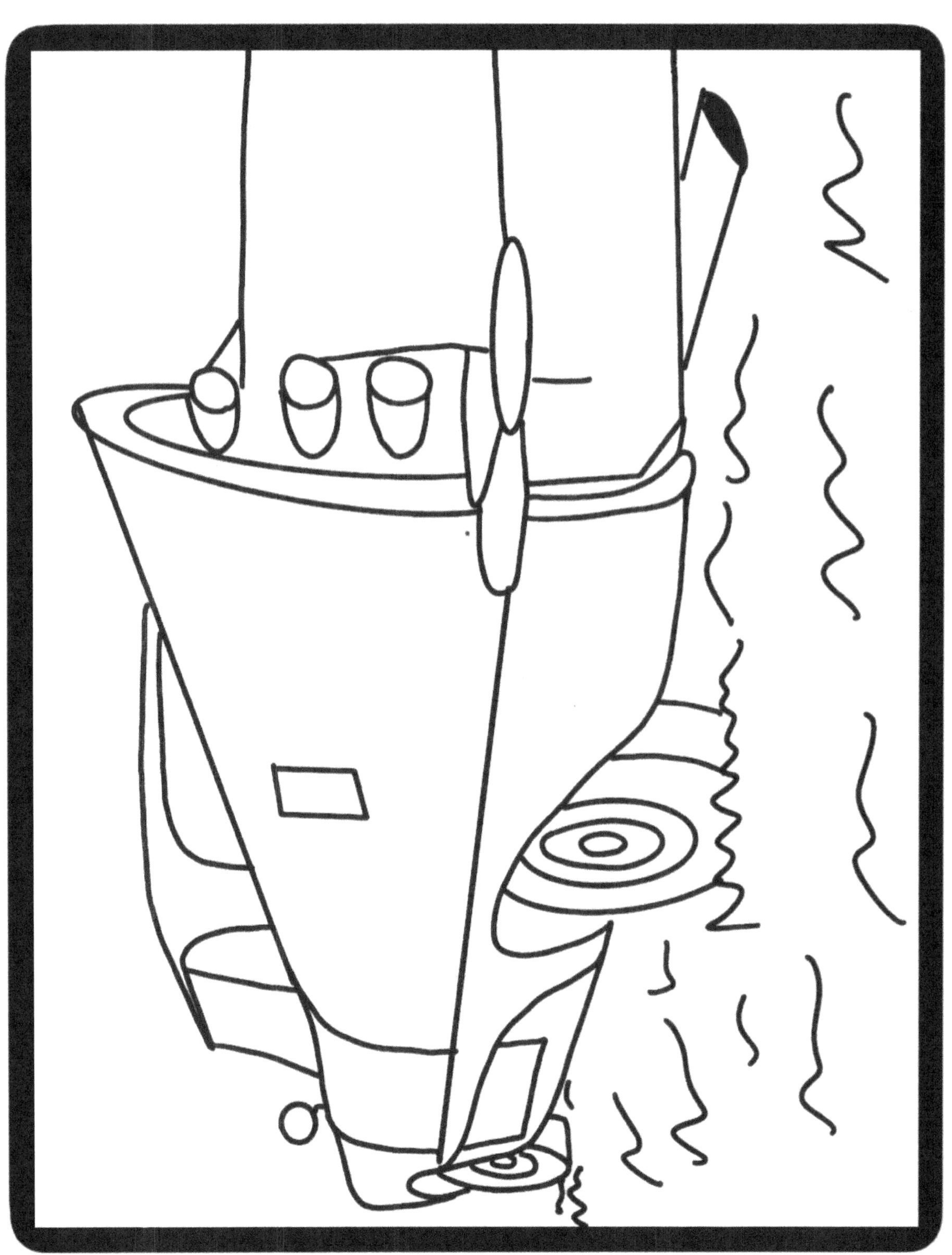

Work on removing yourself from toxic masculinity so you don't have to protect your daughters and sisters from it.

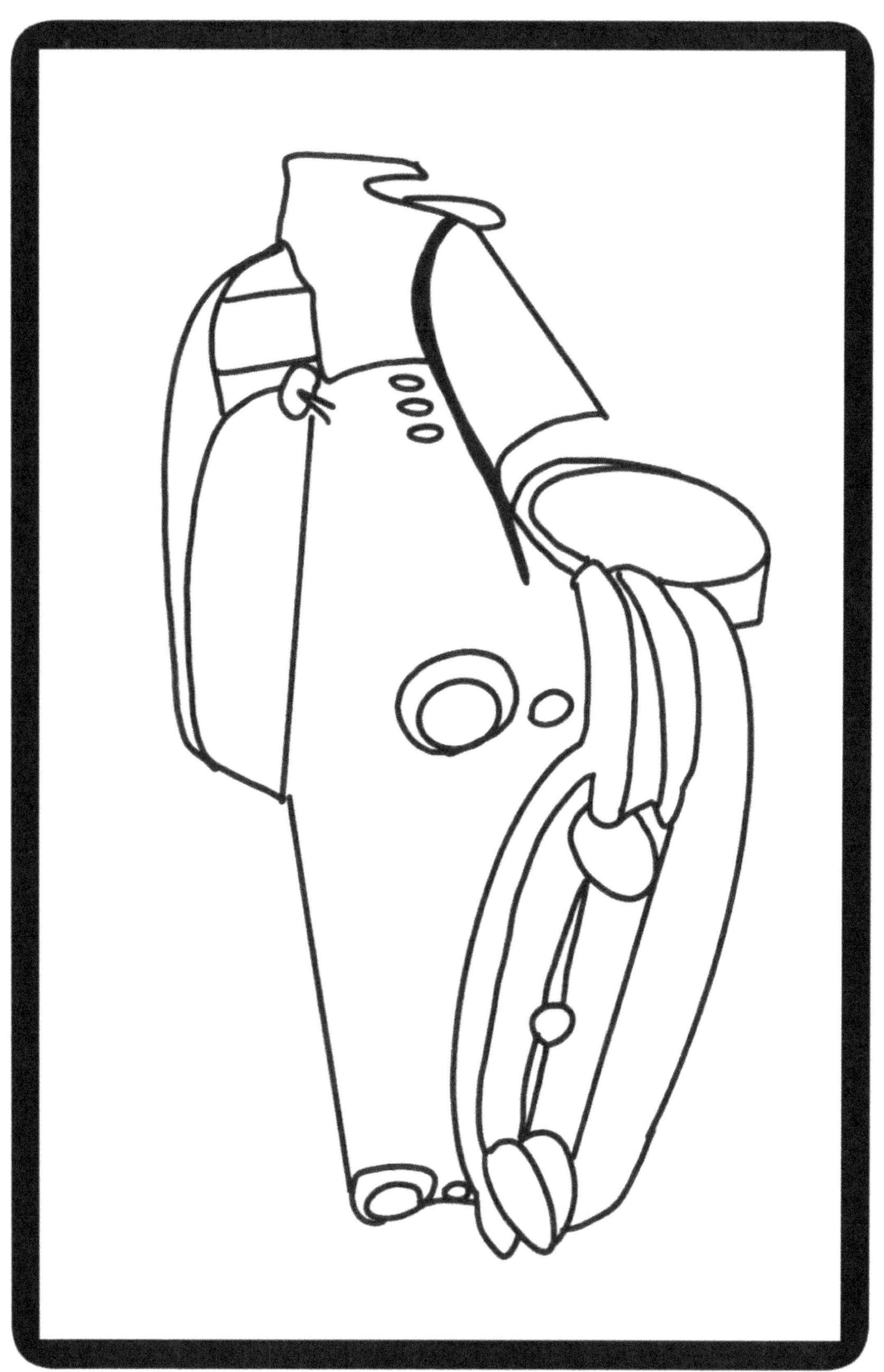

Know that your "no" is valid

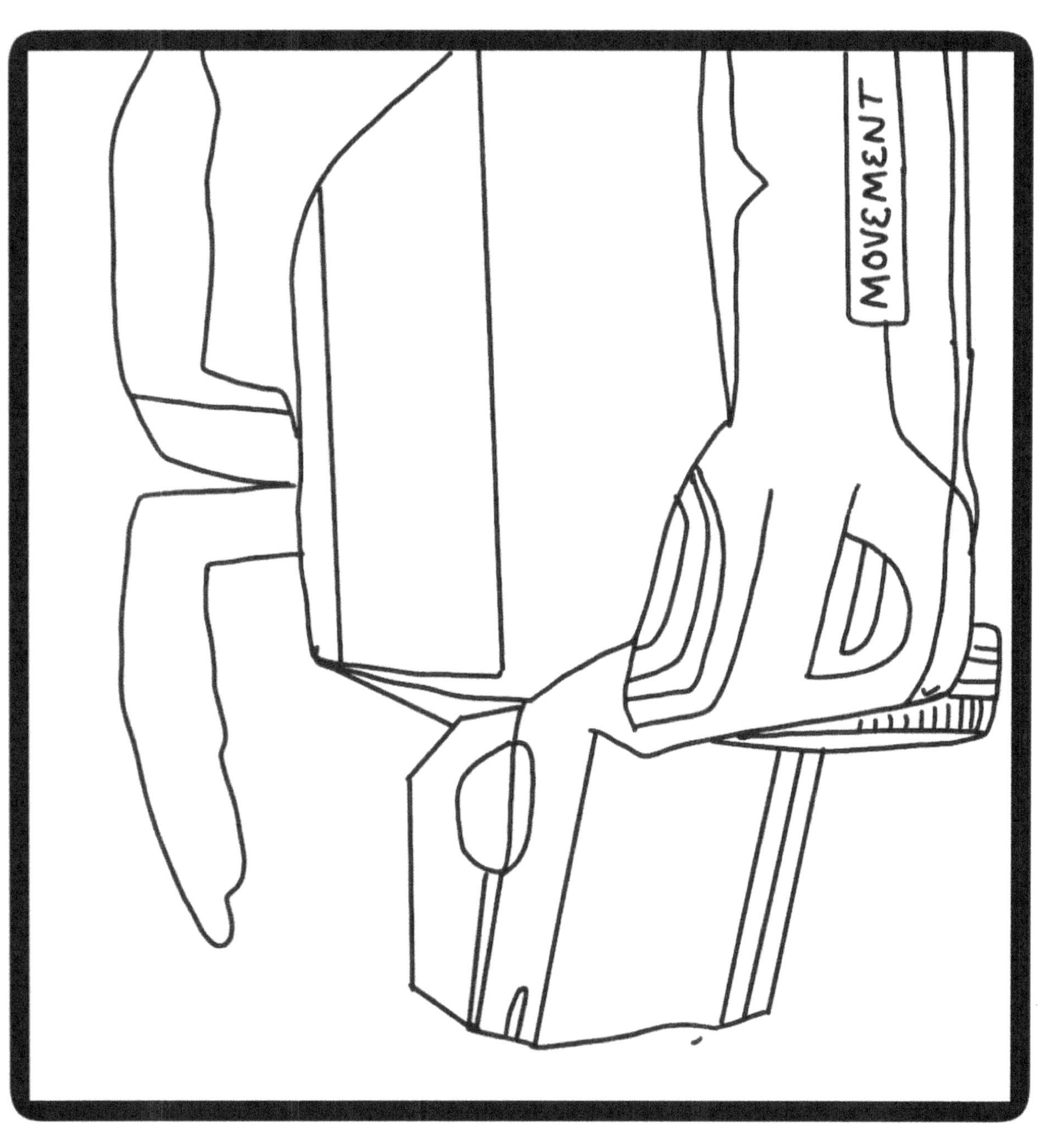

MOVEMENT

Your body is perfect the way it is

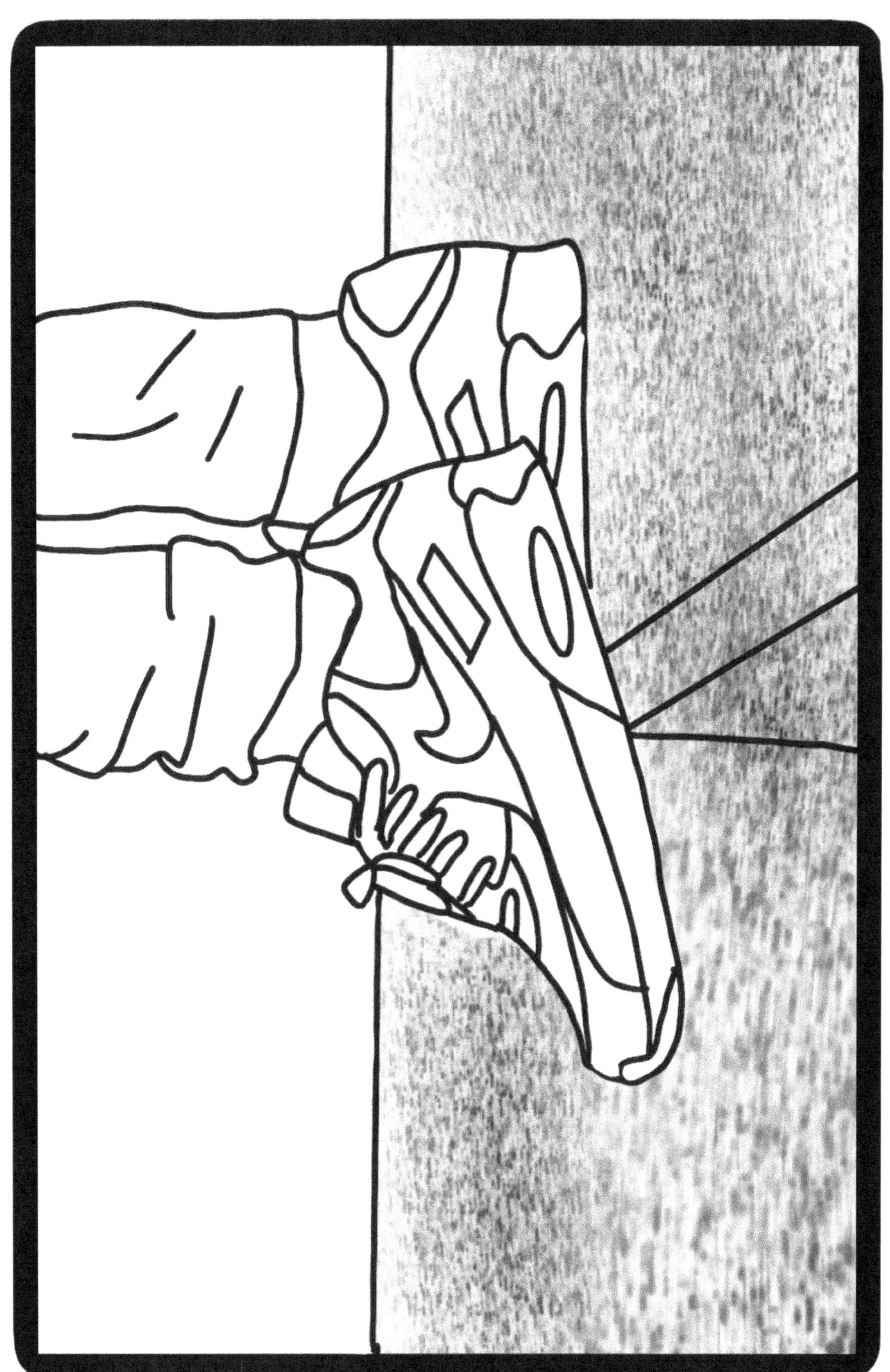

Your freedom of creativity matters

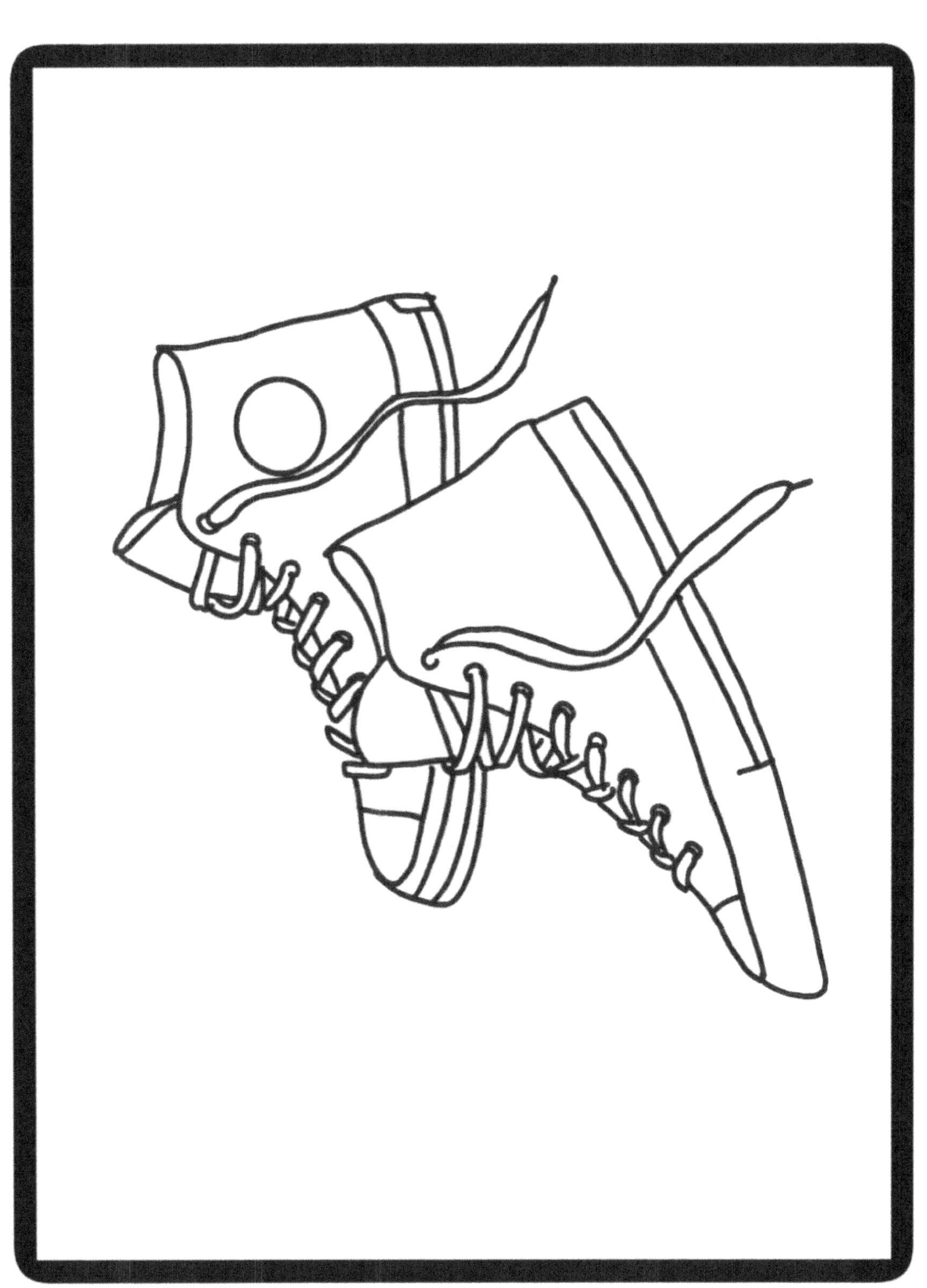

Words from Men Fighting Along with You:

At times it may feel that you are in this constant state of fighting, and at times that may be the truth. In your life, you will have to battle the world, yourself, and racism. You will find yourself stuck in these cracks of life where you may feel that you fall in so chaotically. You are in control of your own life. You are worth your life. Whenever you are struggling please remember that you are surrounded by black men and women who will love you. Never stop working on bettering yourself because it is a constant goal that we must take the initiative to achieve.

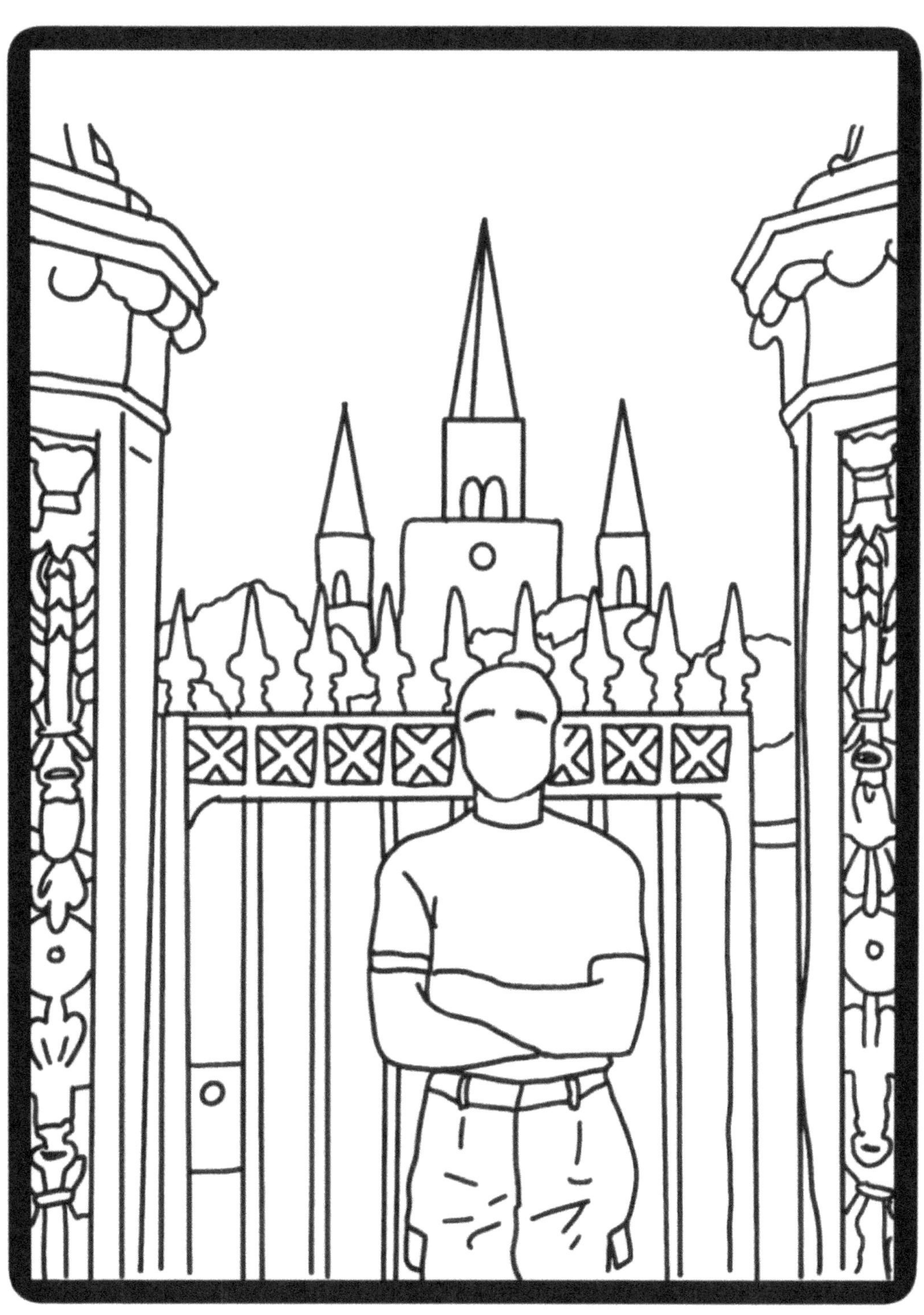

Find peace in knowing wherever you are…there is someone in this world who sees you and loves you

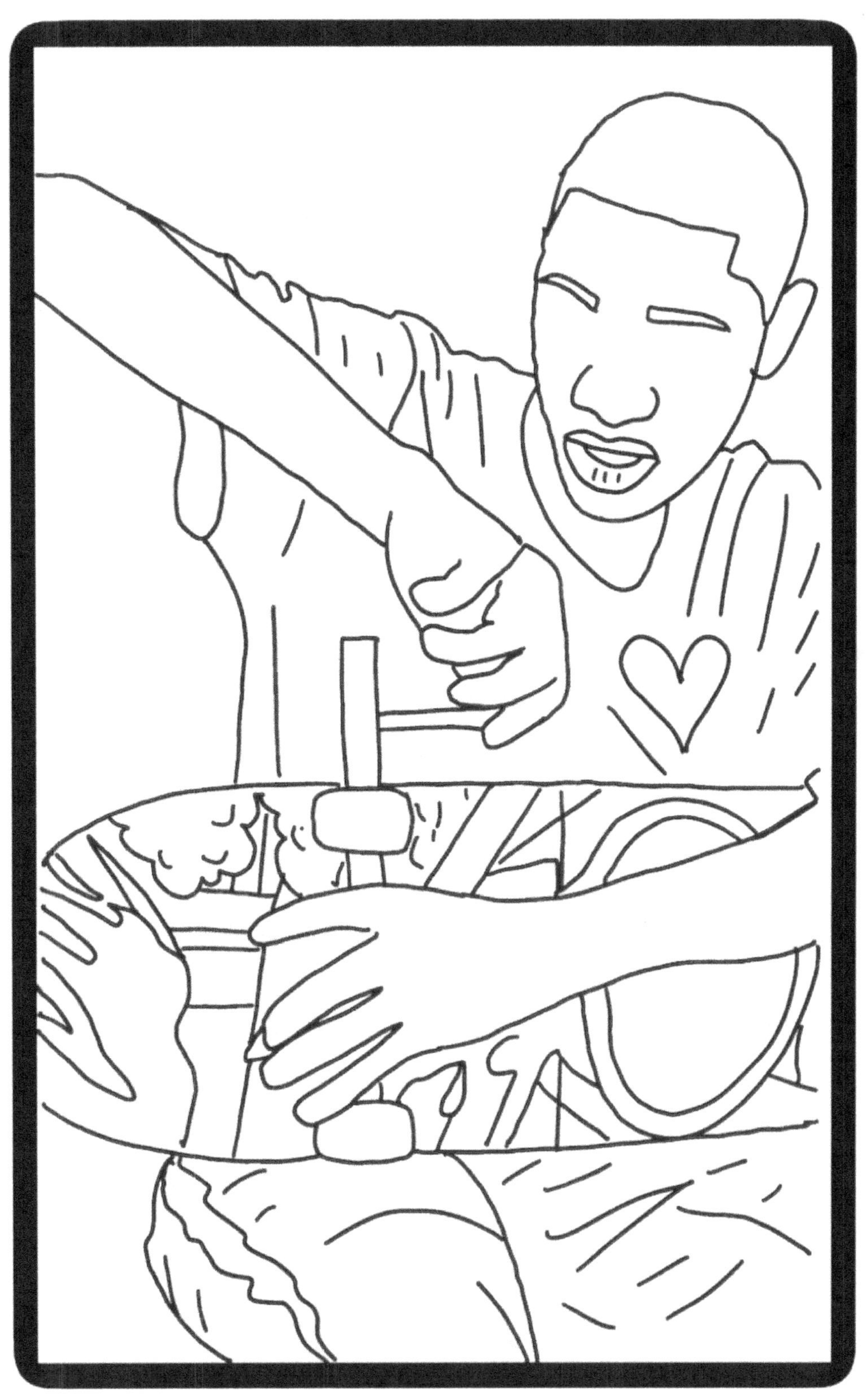

You are not the leaders of tomorrow…where you stand right now is your domain and you are the leader.

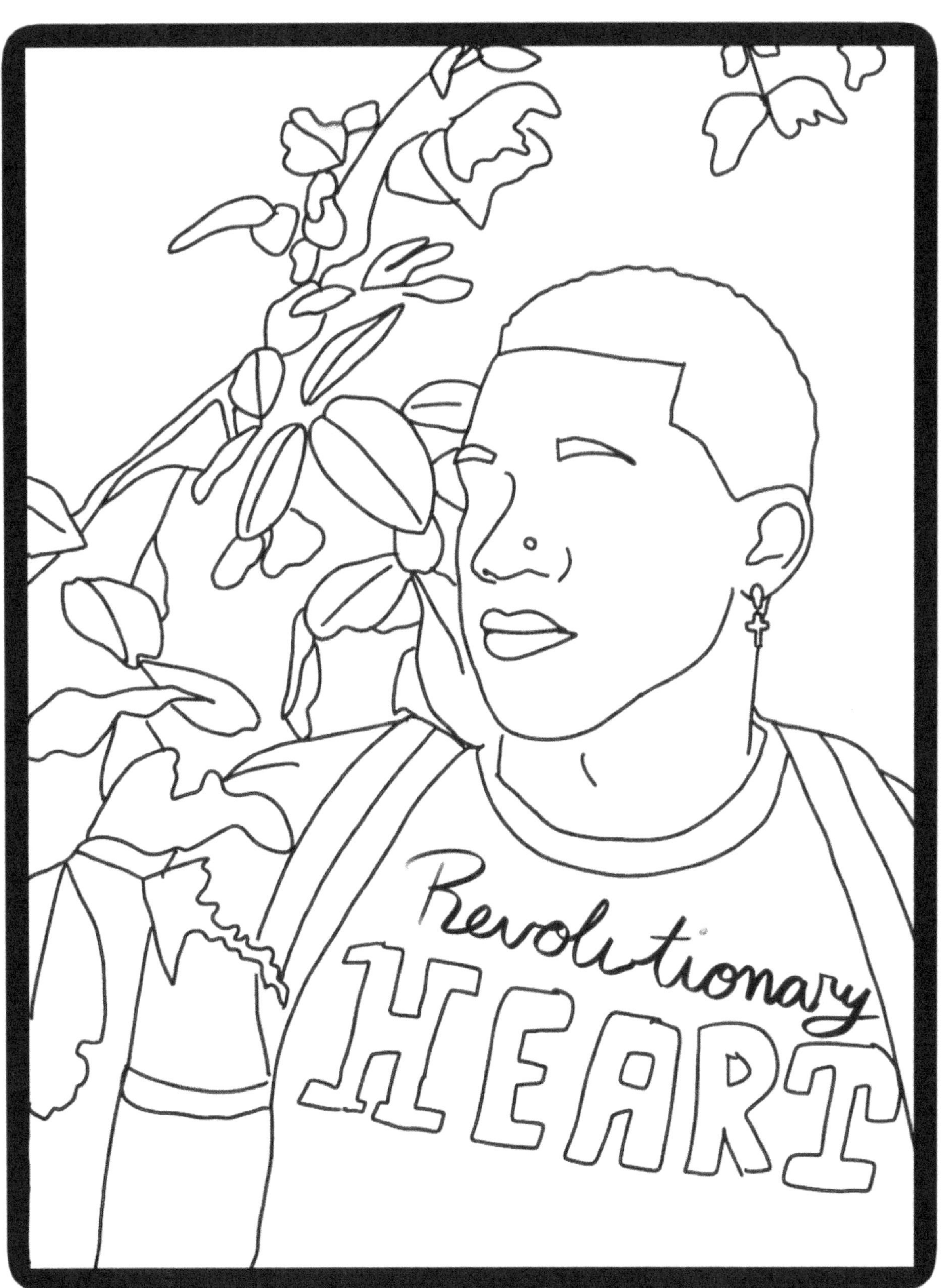

Revolutionary
HEART

Someone is always watching you so don't get discouraged. You always have someone looking out for you and looking up to you

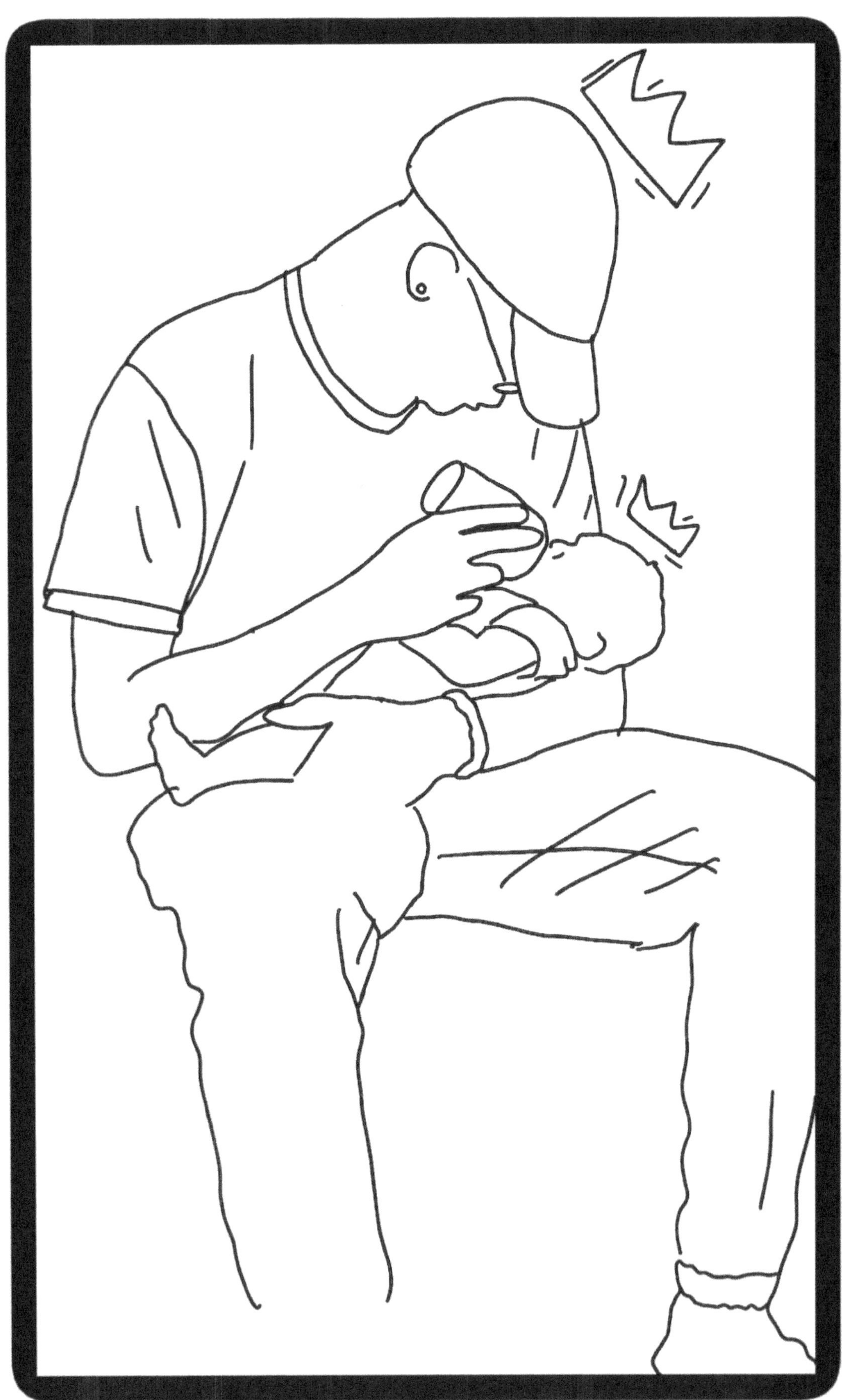

Protect the Black Women in your Life

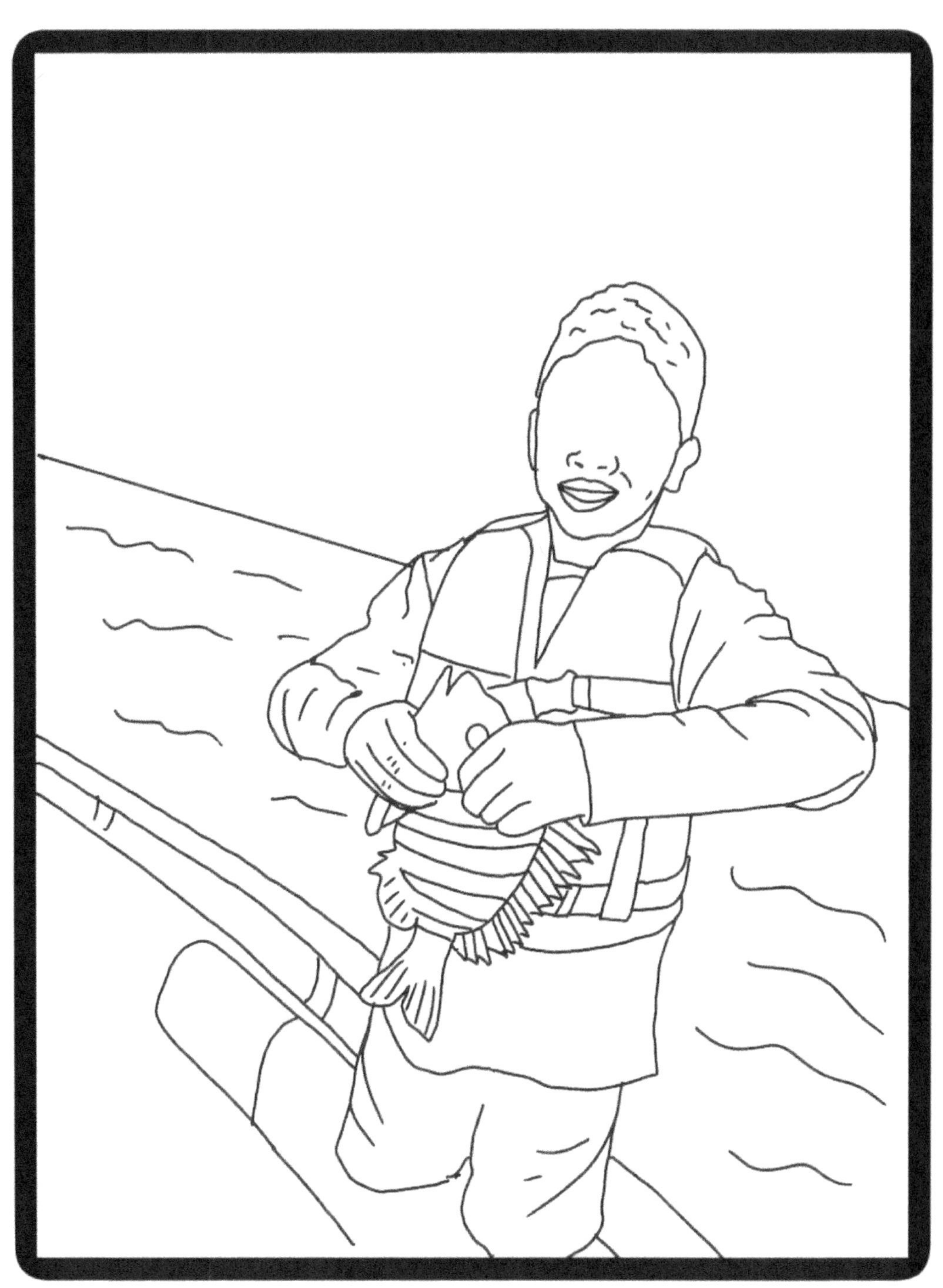

Learn from the Black Women in your life

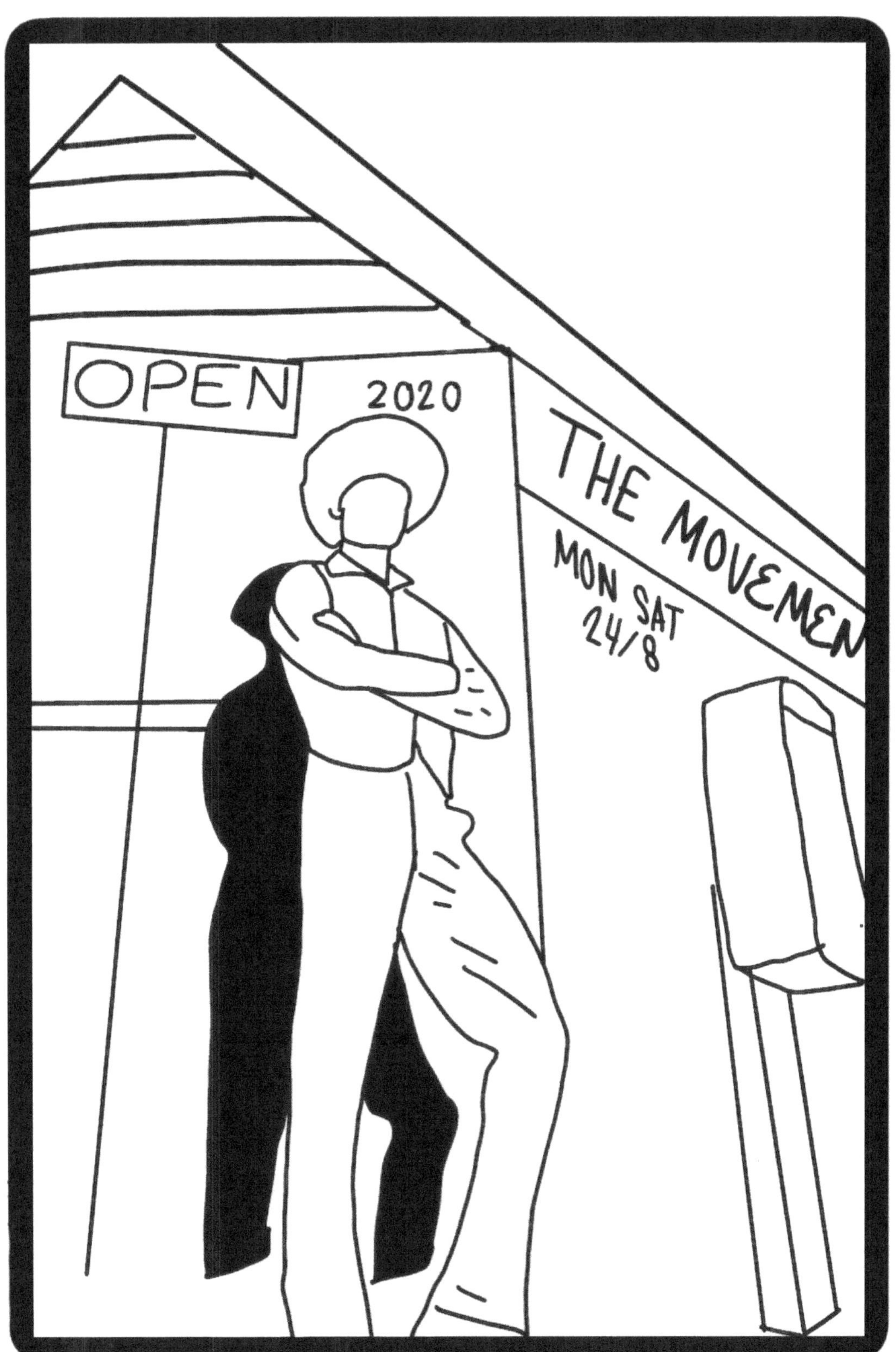

OPEN
2020
THE MOVEMEN
MON SAT
24/8

Your pain is valid.

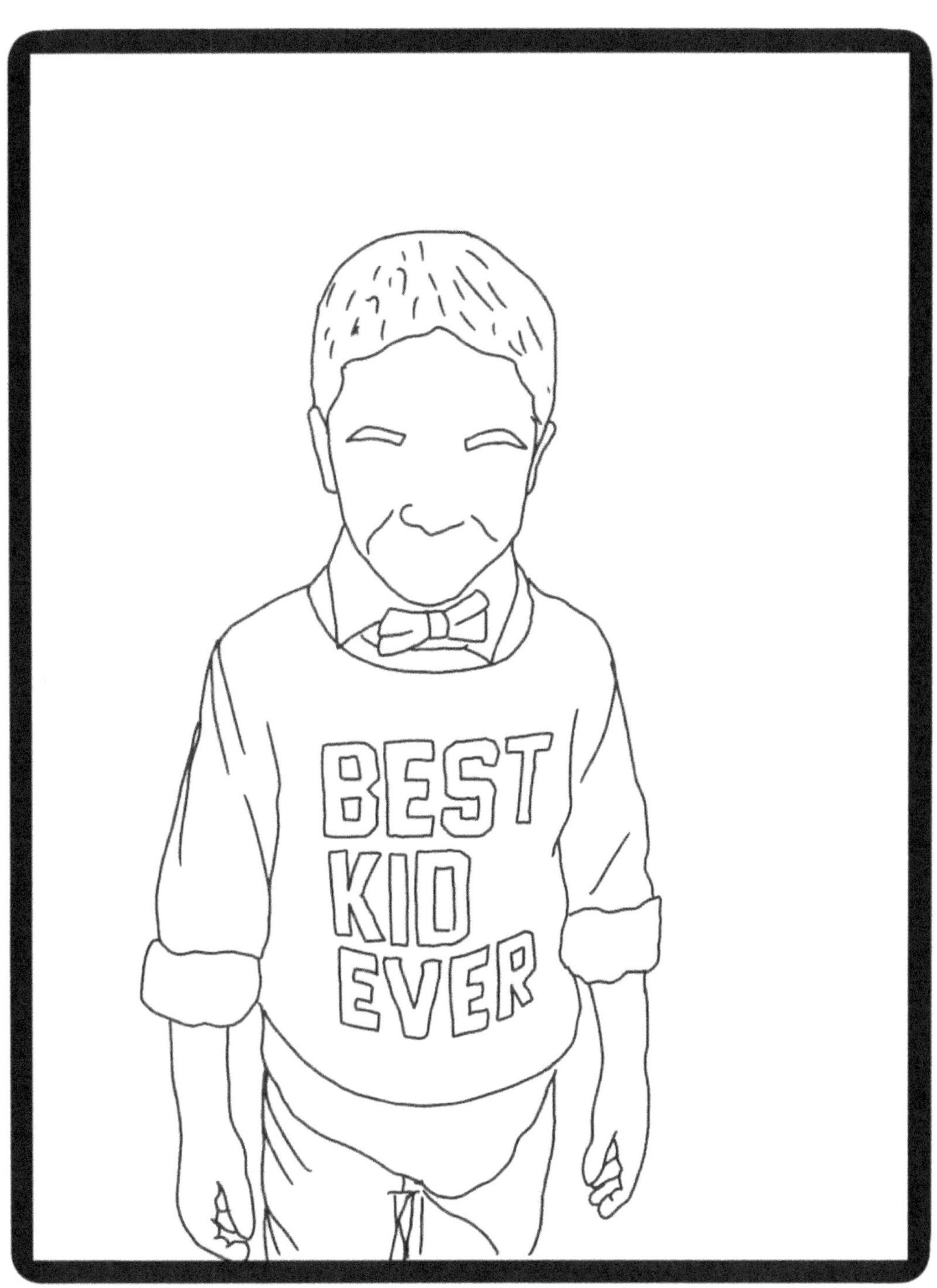

BEST
KID
EVER

Everyone has dreams so don't let anyone tell you that yours are out of reach

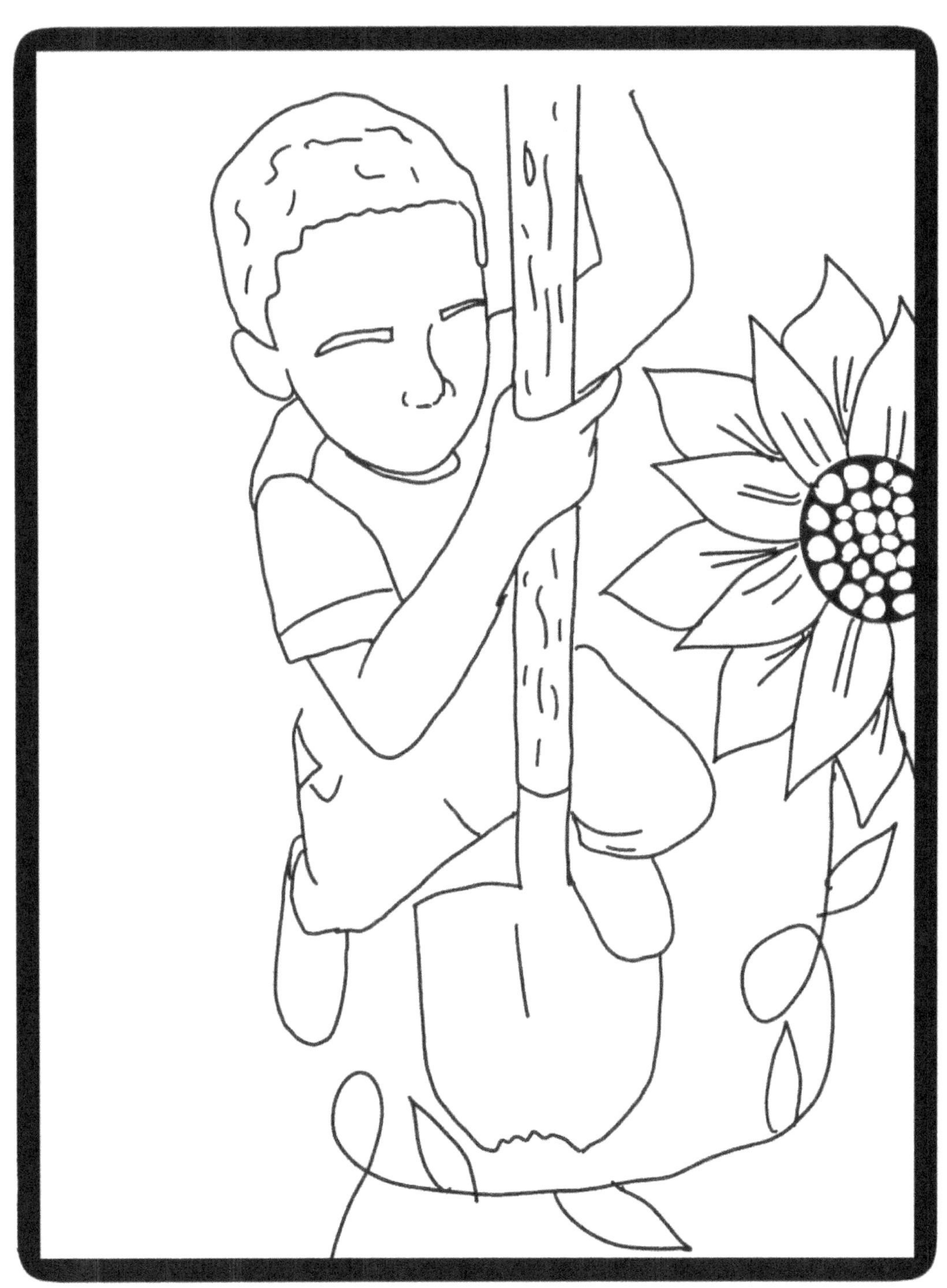

Take a breath, go outside, and release
the tension from the day.

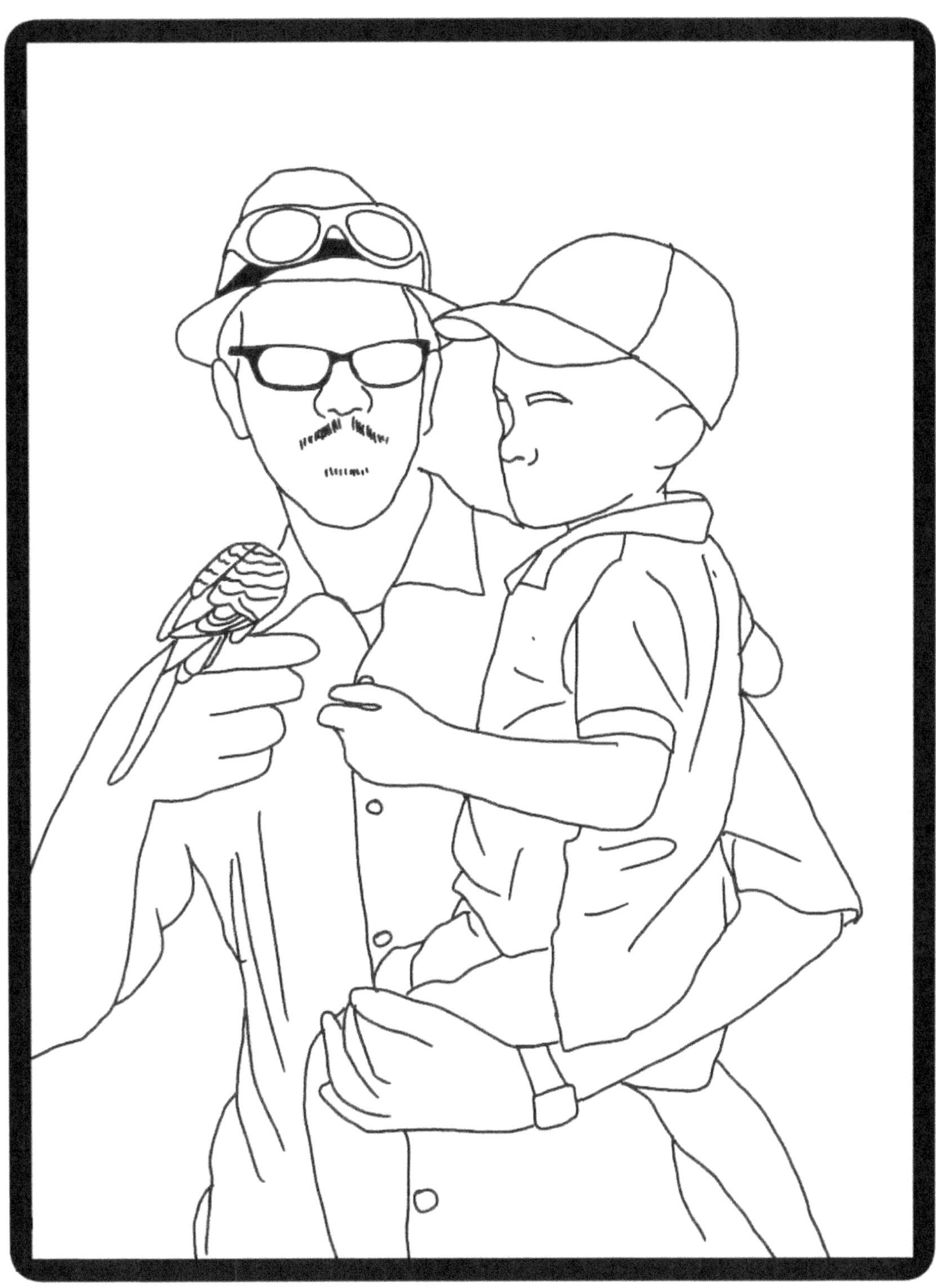

You deserve to be loved.

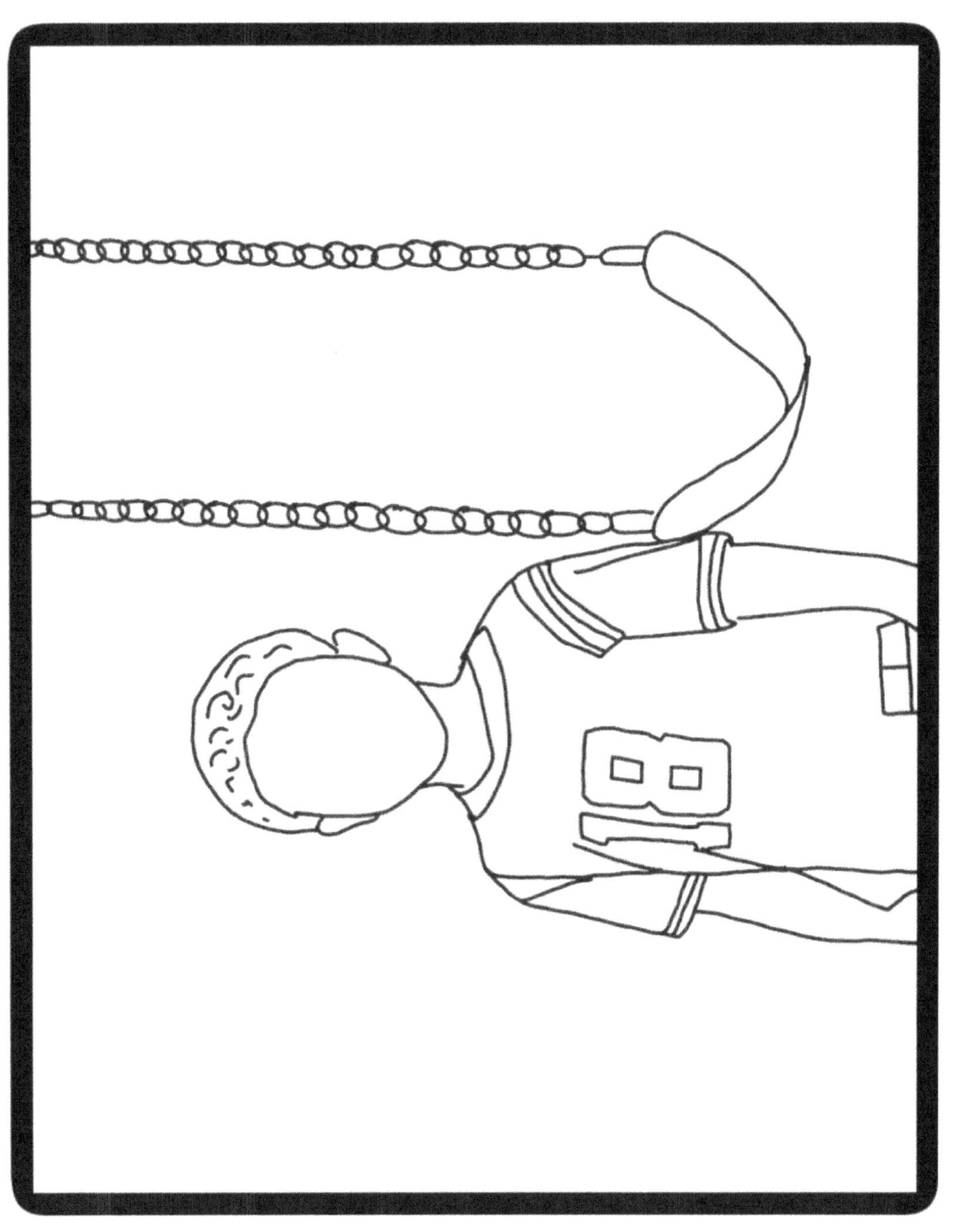

Your life matters.

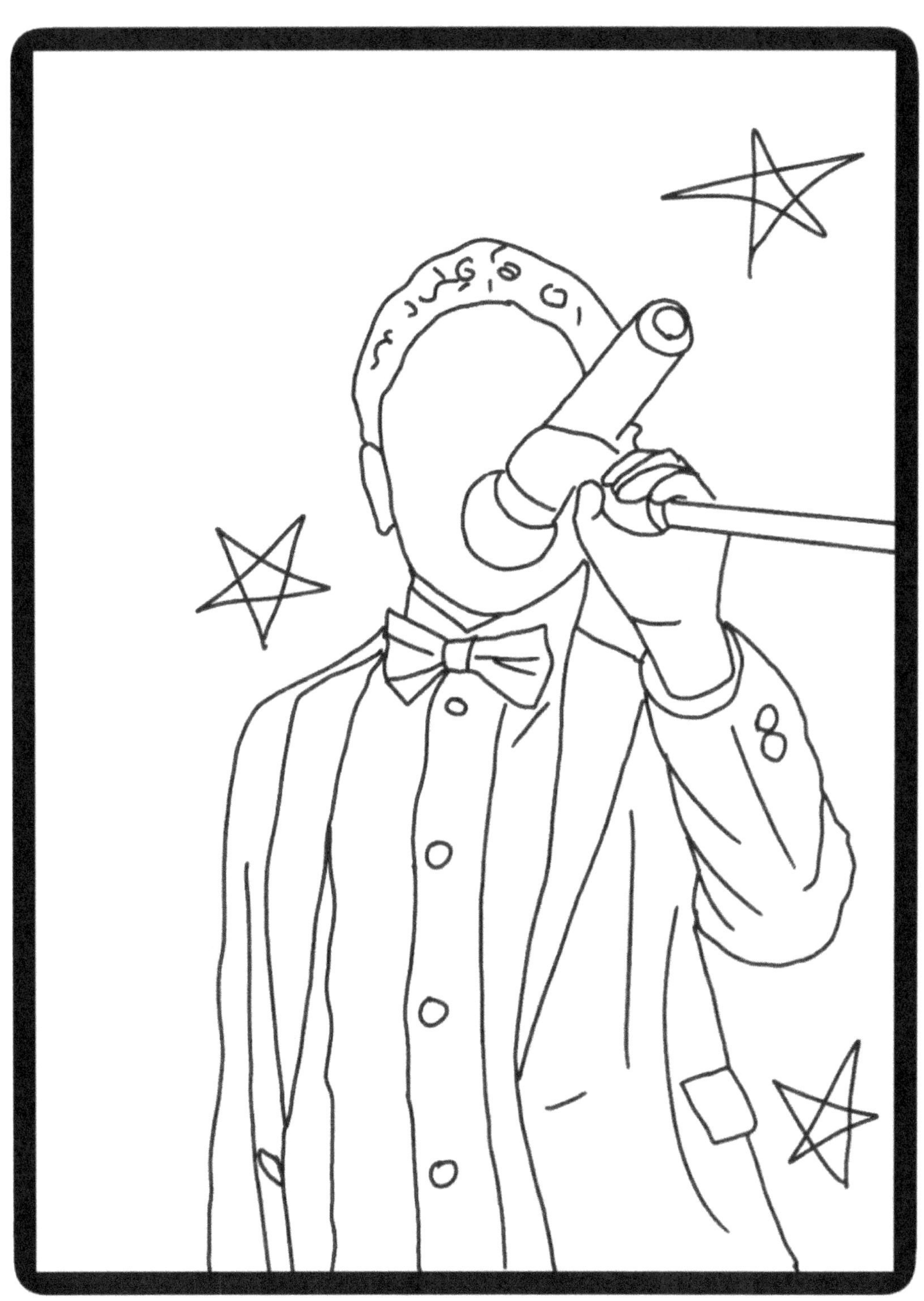

Being feminine doesn't make you less
of a man.

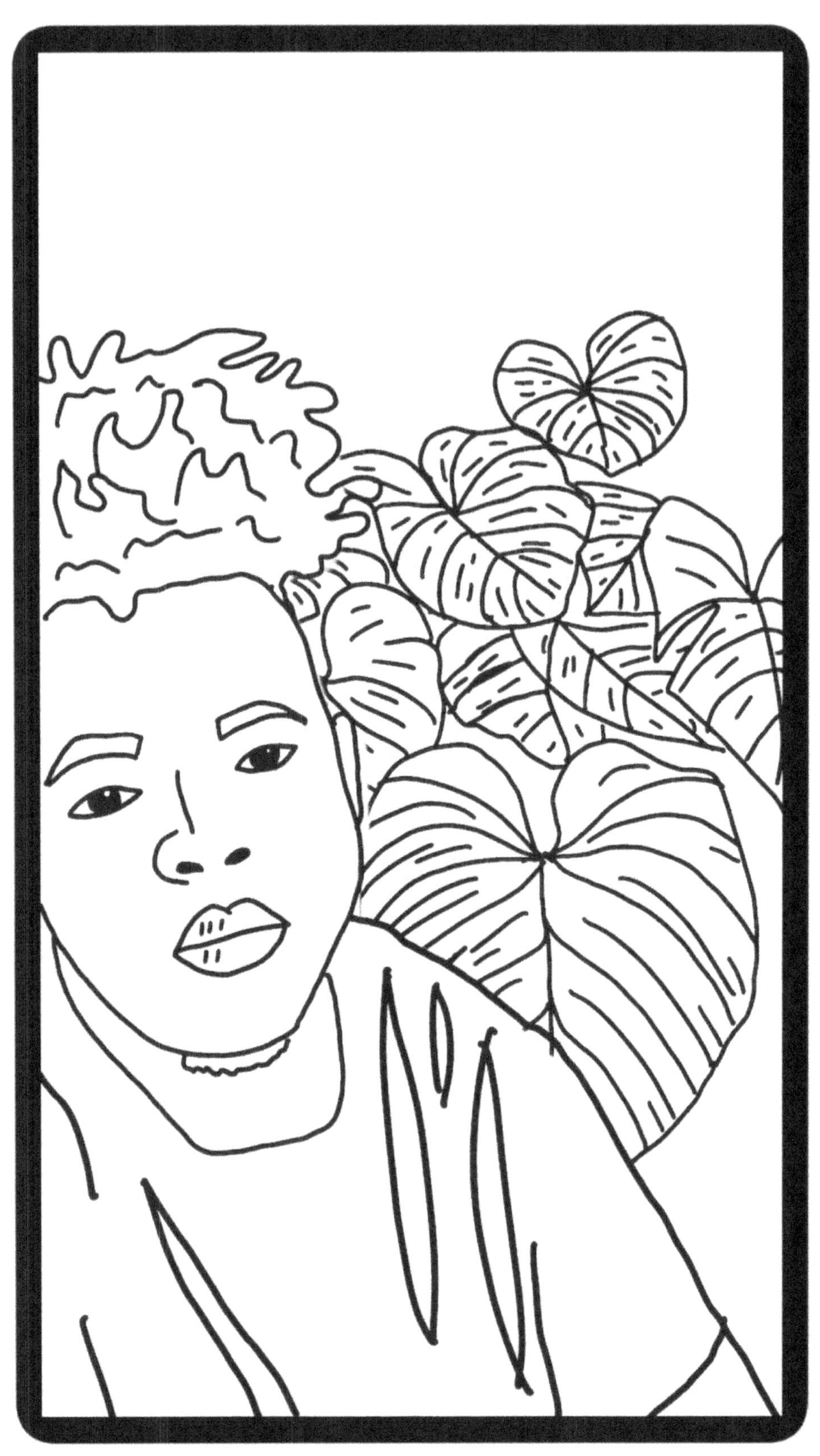

You matter.

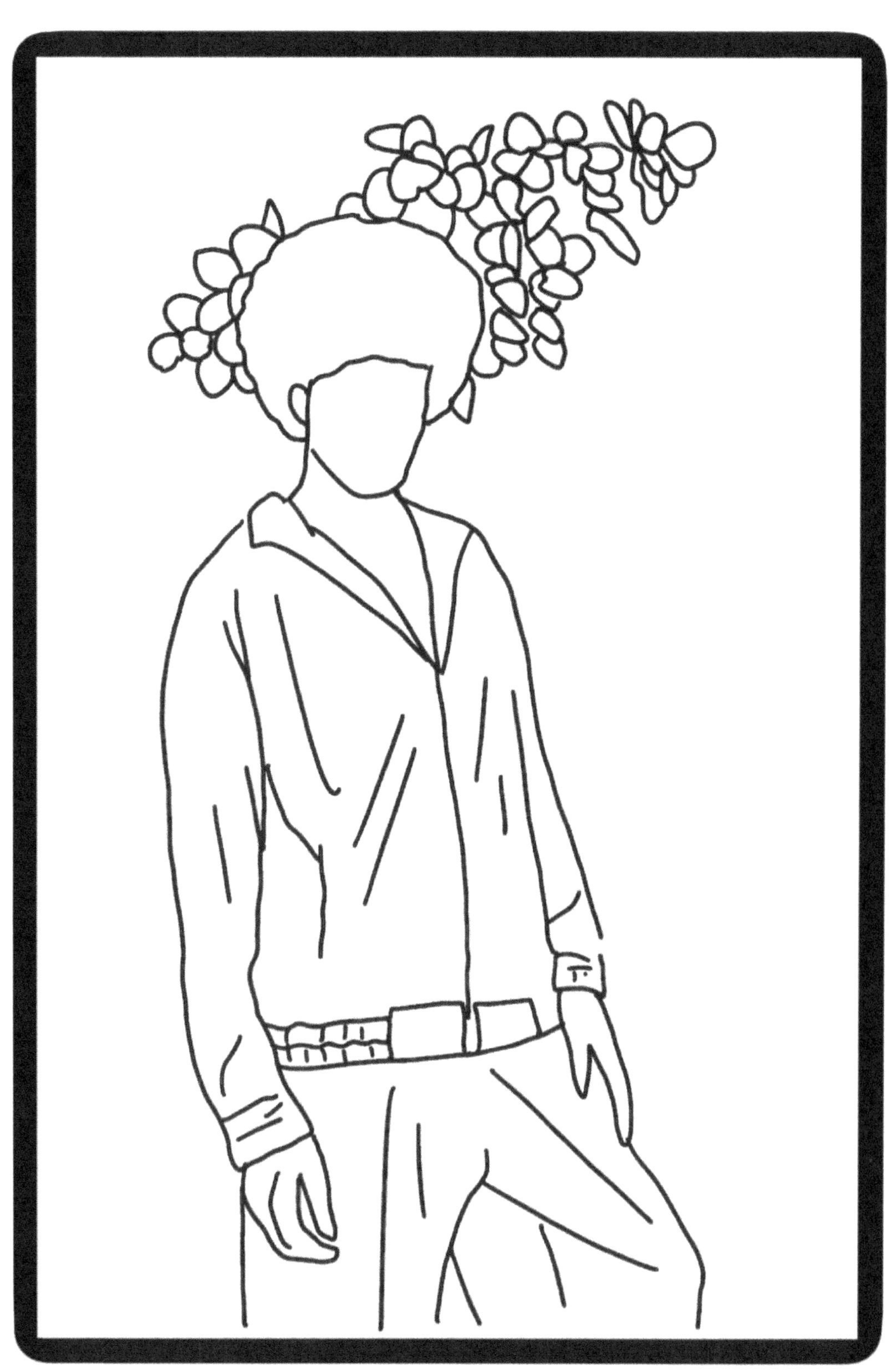

Cherish the Black Women in your
Life

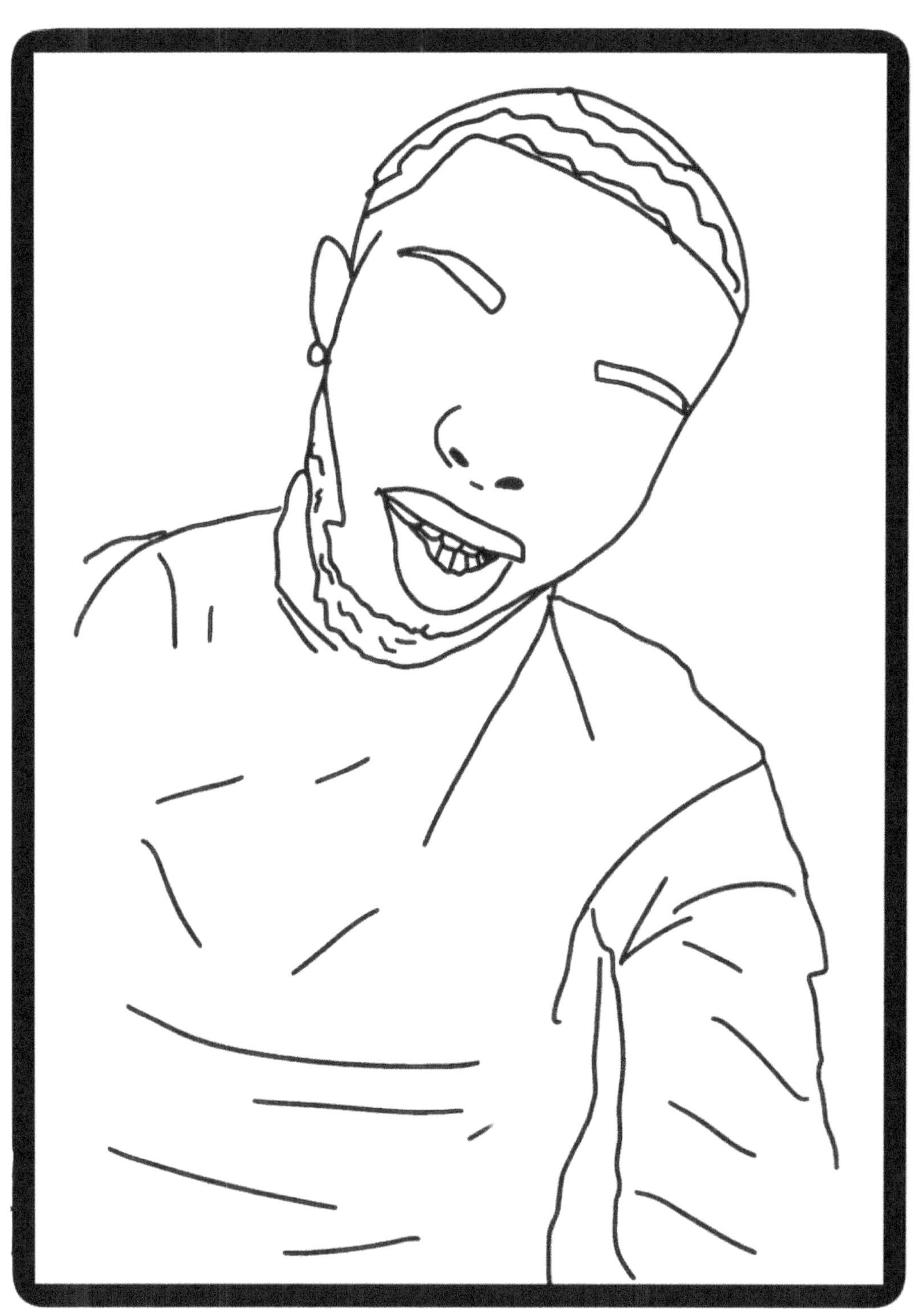

Value the Black Women in your life

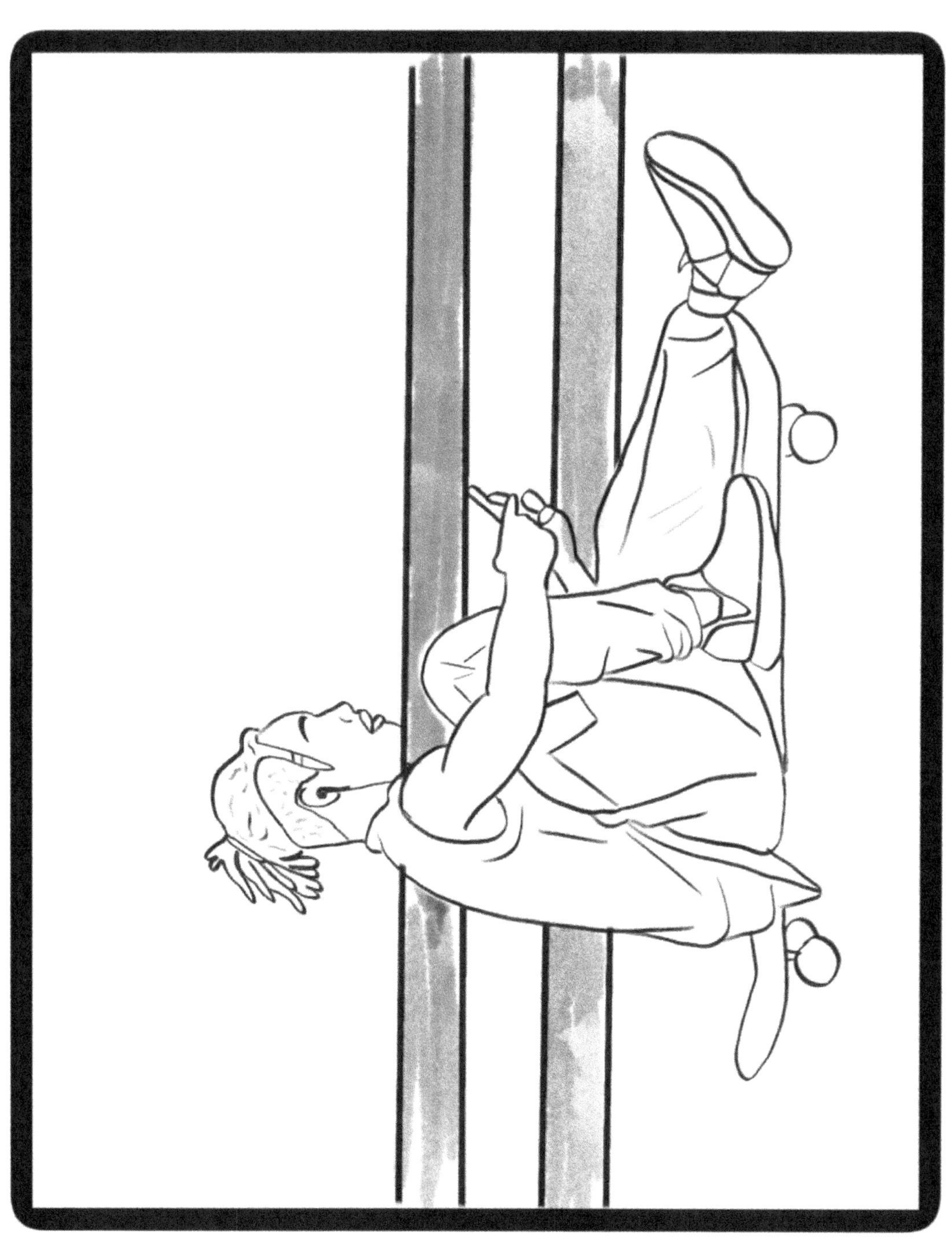

You deserve to be able to let your
guard down

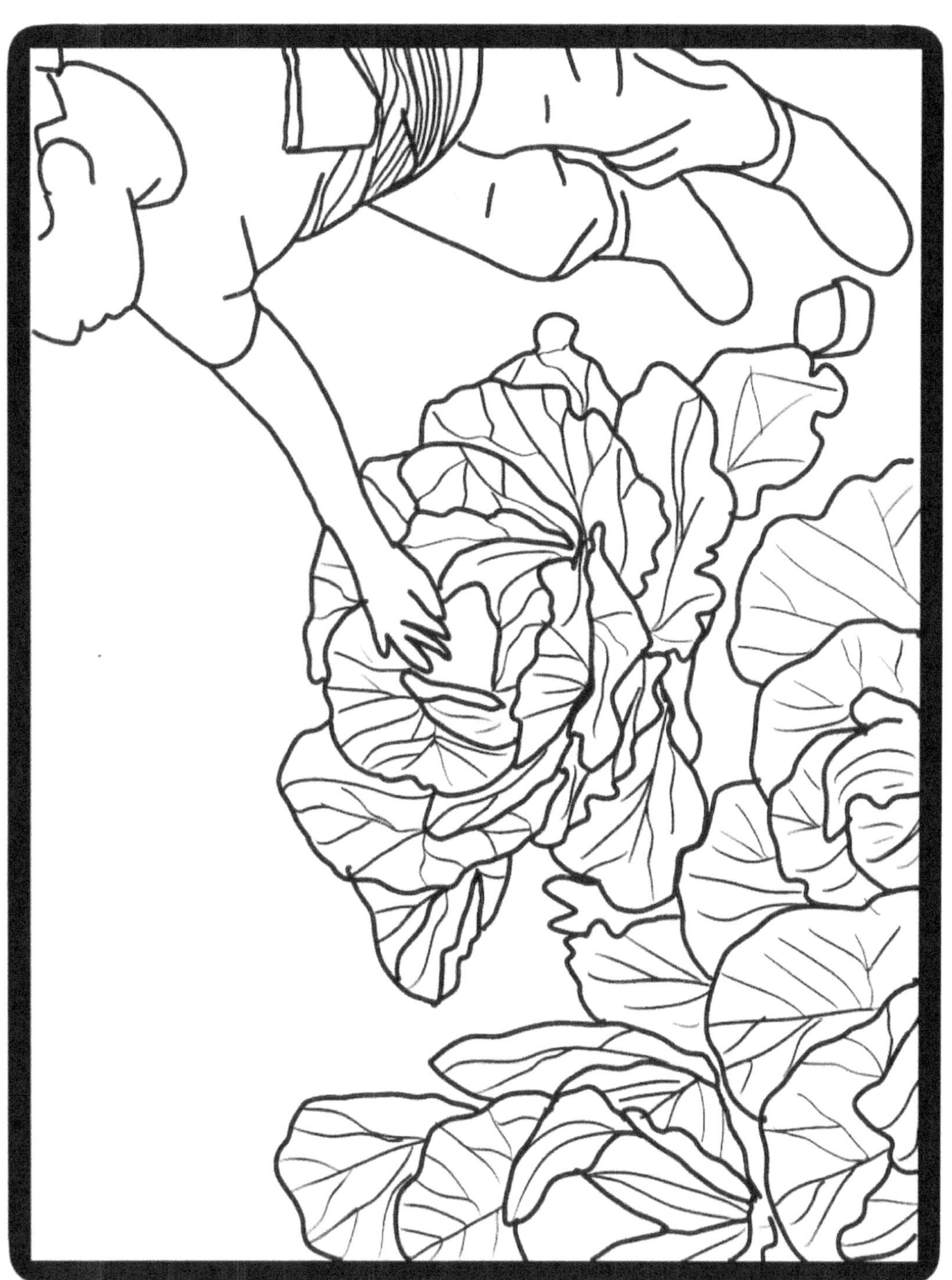

Your hair is beautiful.

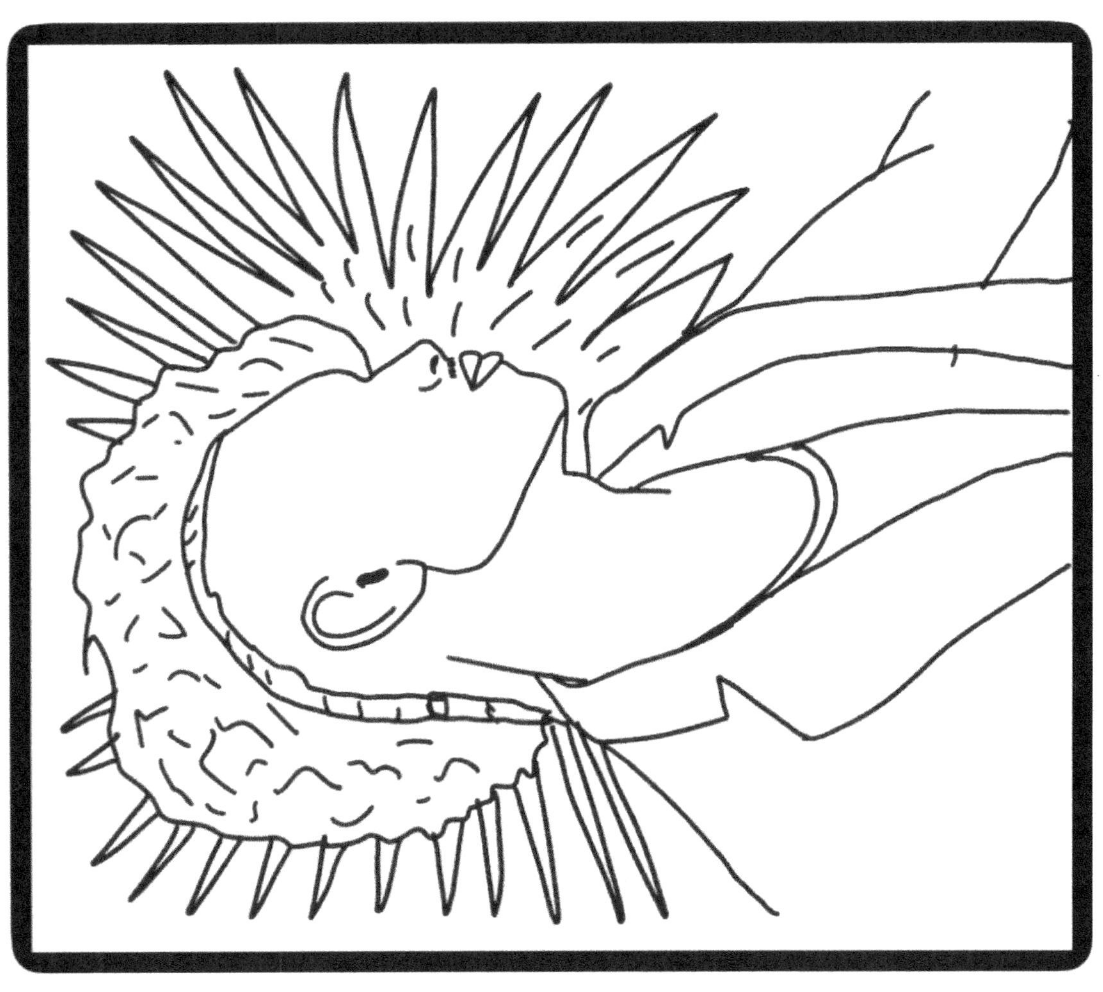

Don't stop when it gets hard just work
harder until it gets done

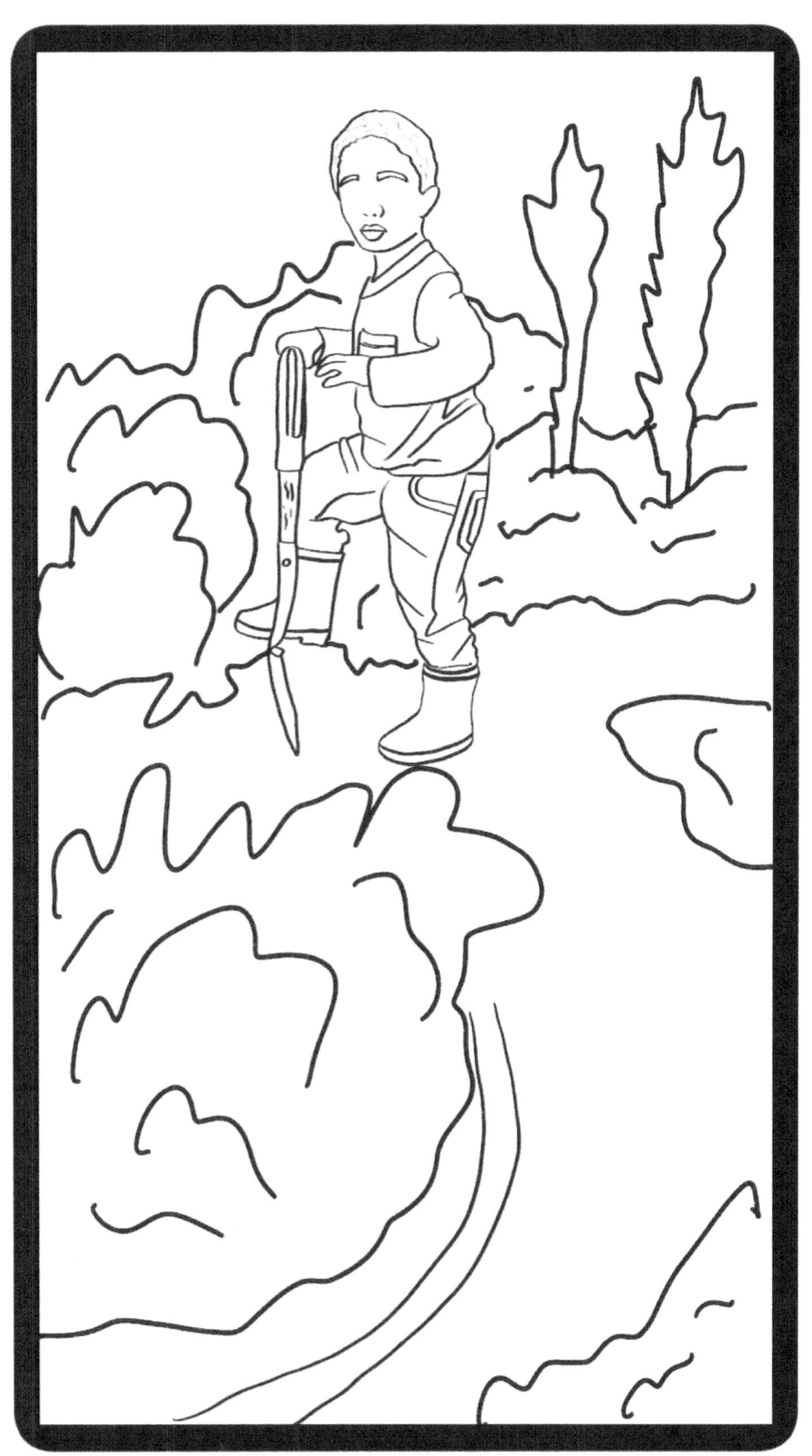

Even when the world is against you
remember that you are not alone.

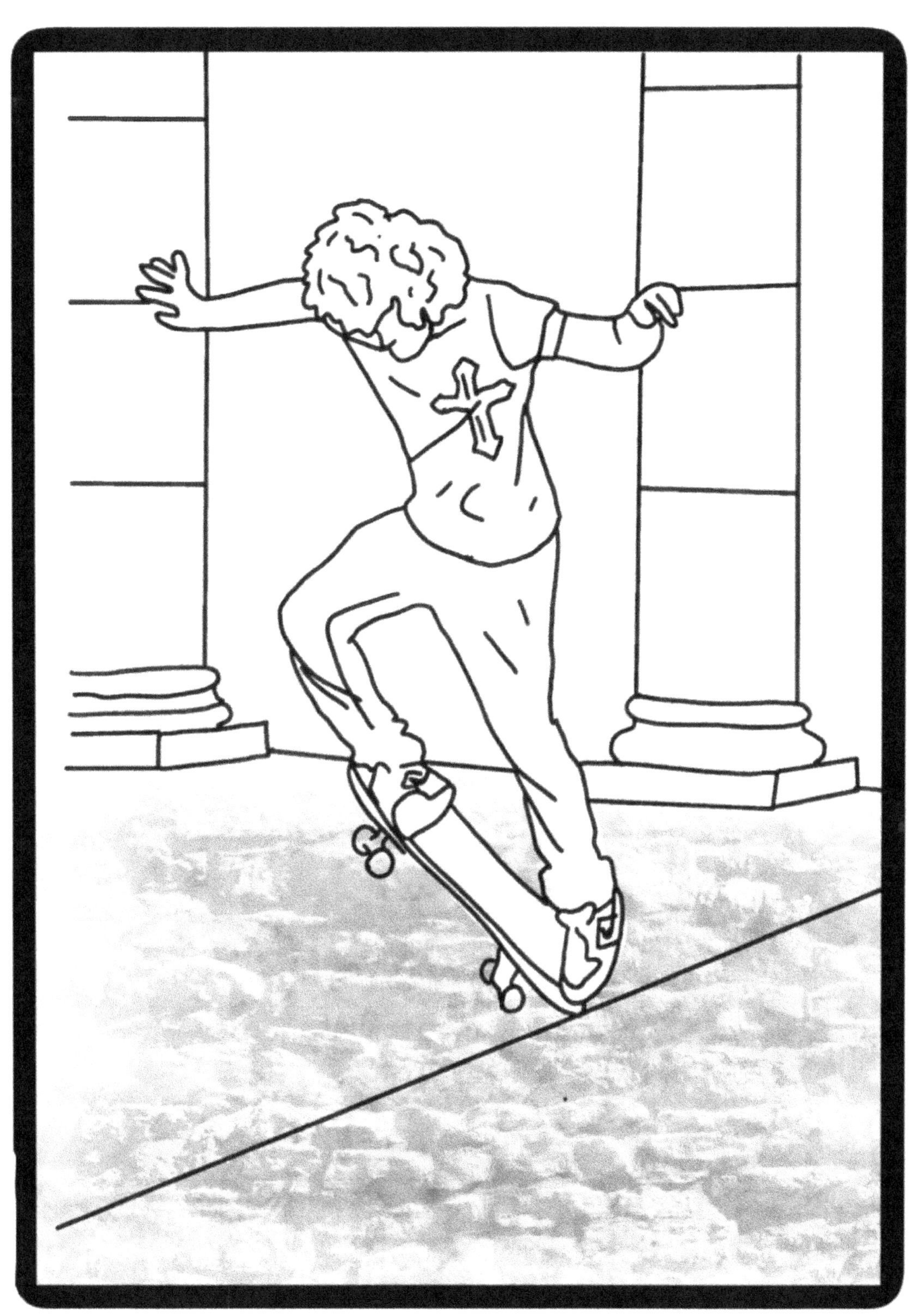

The world needs people like you in it

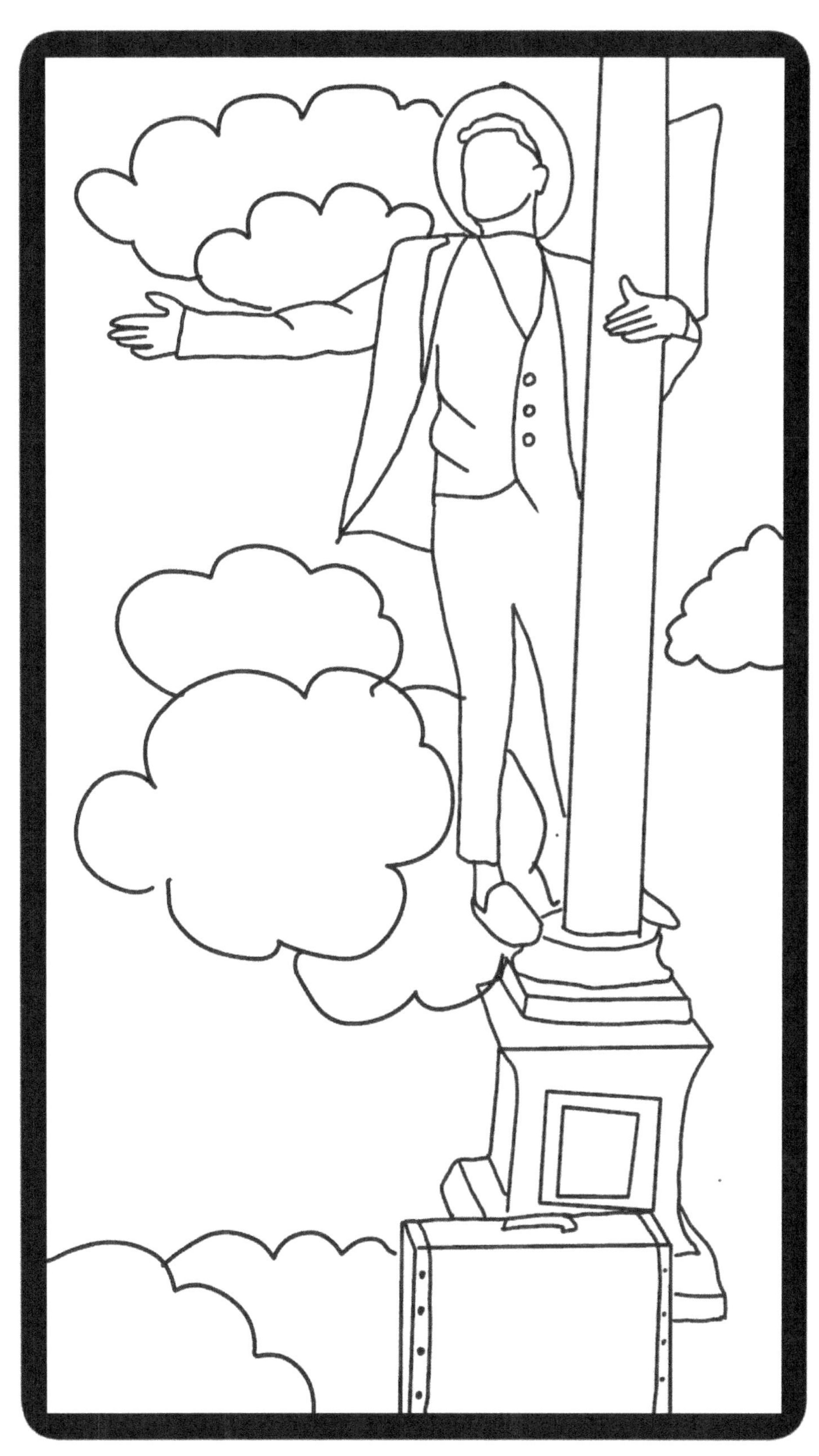

You are needed in this world

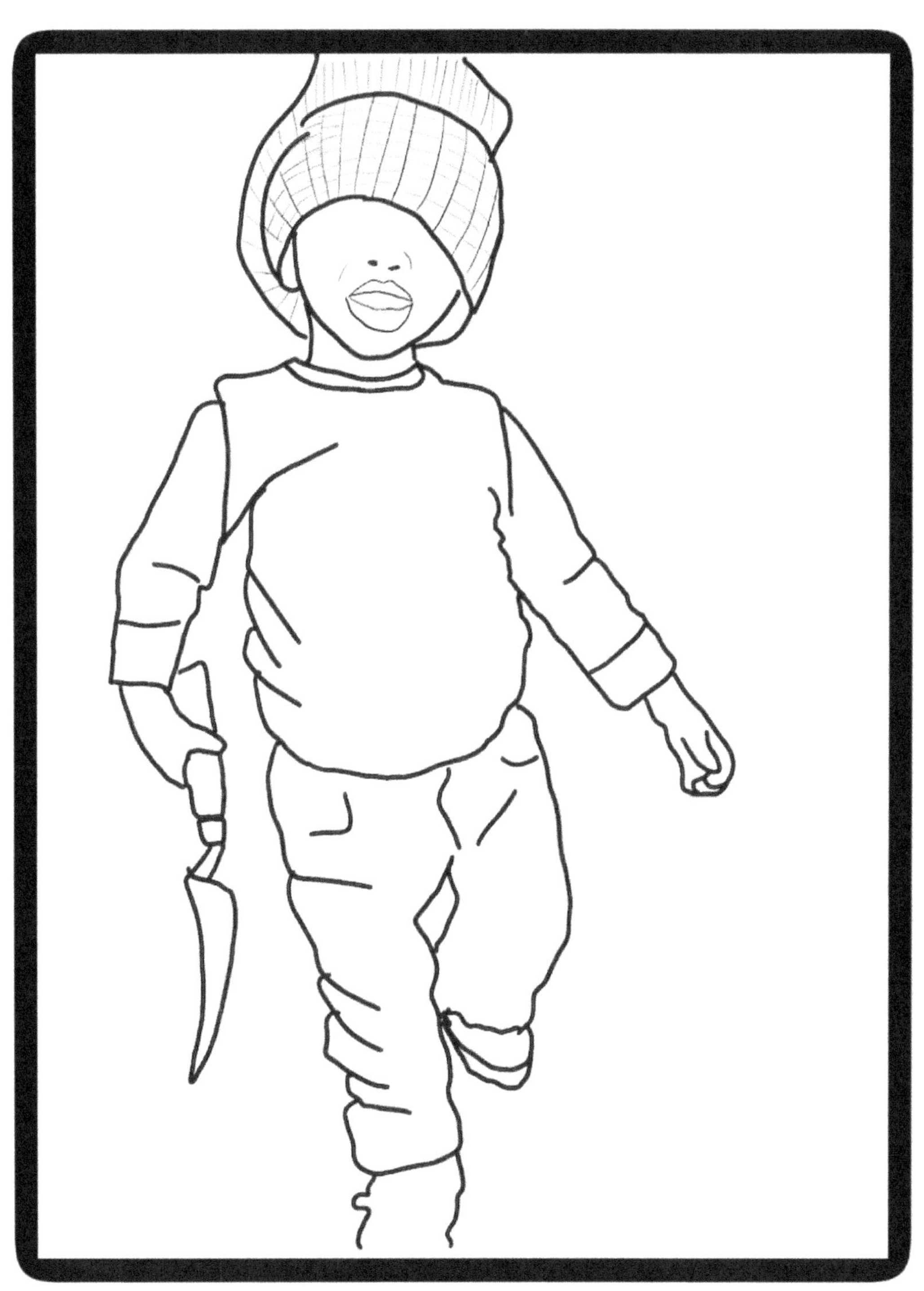

Love is not to be feared but rather
treasured

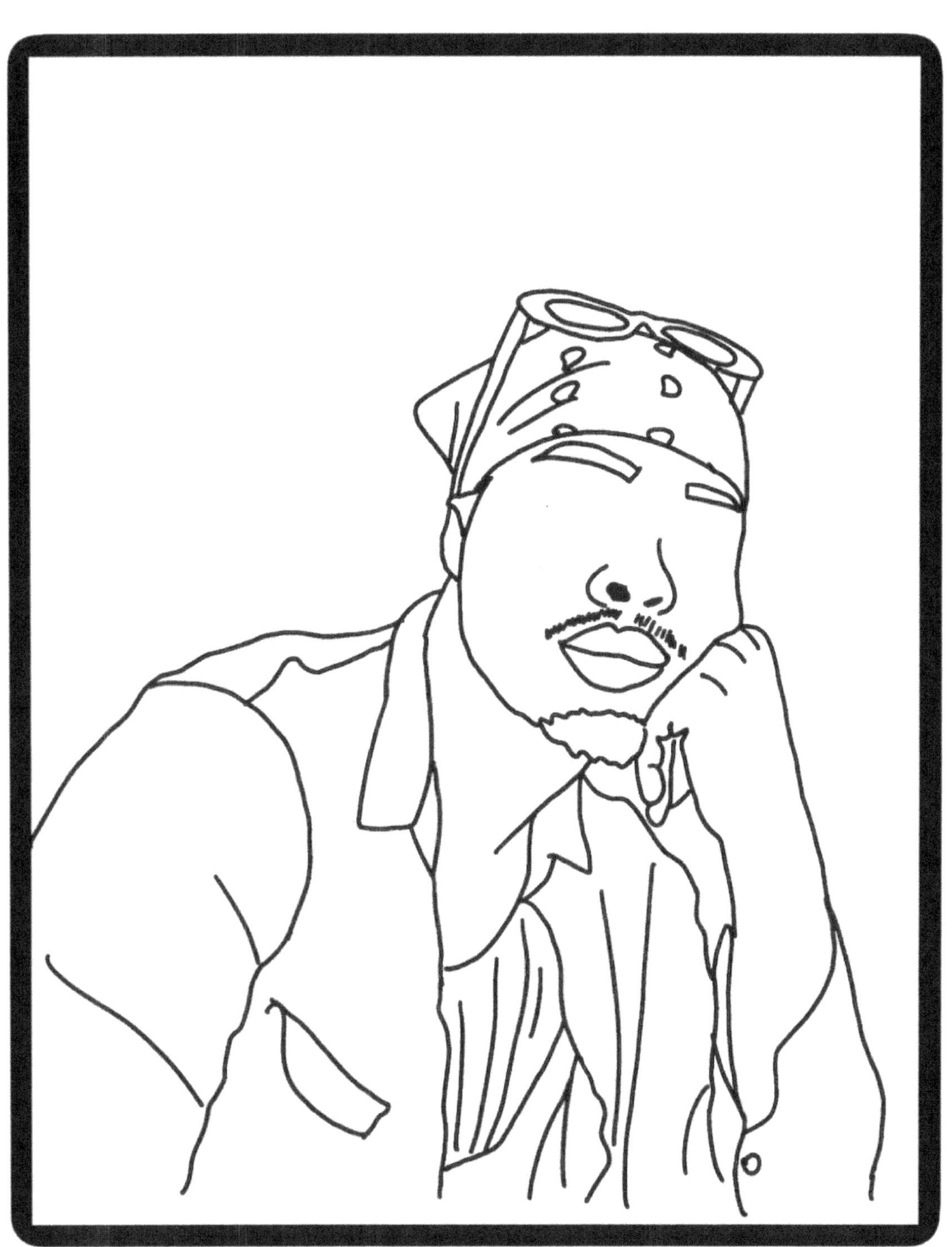

Your freedom of creativity matters

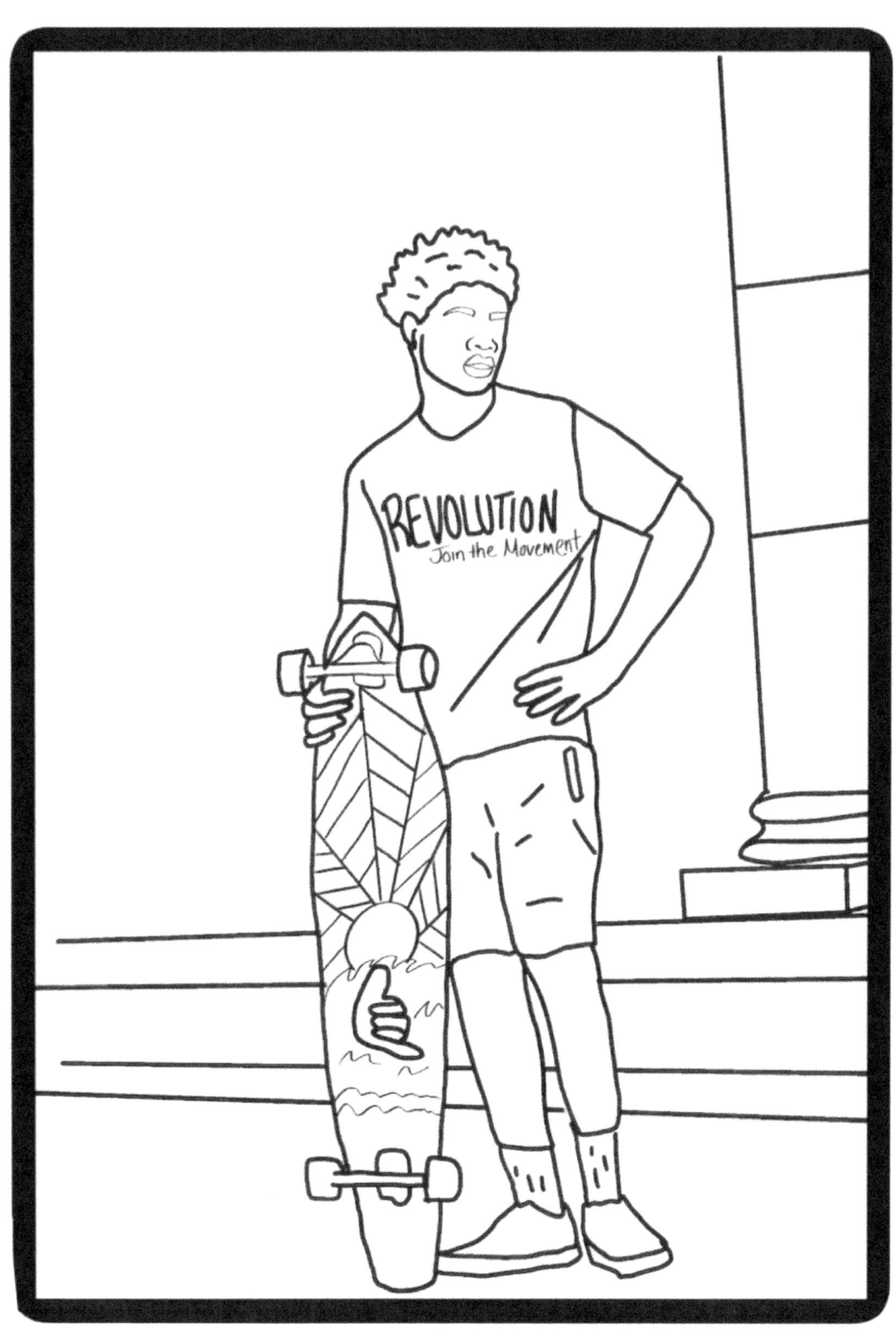
REVOLUTION
Join the Movement

You are enough.

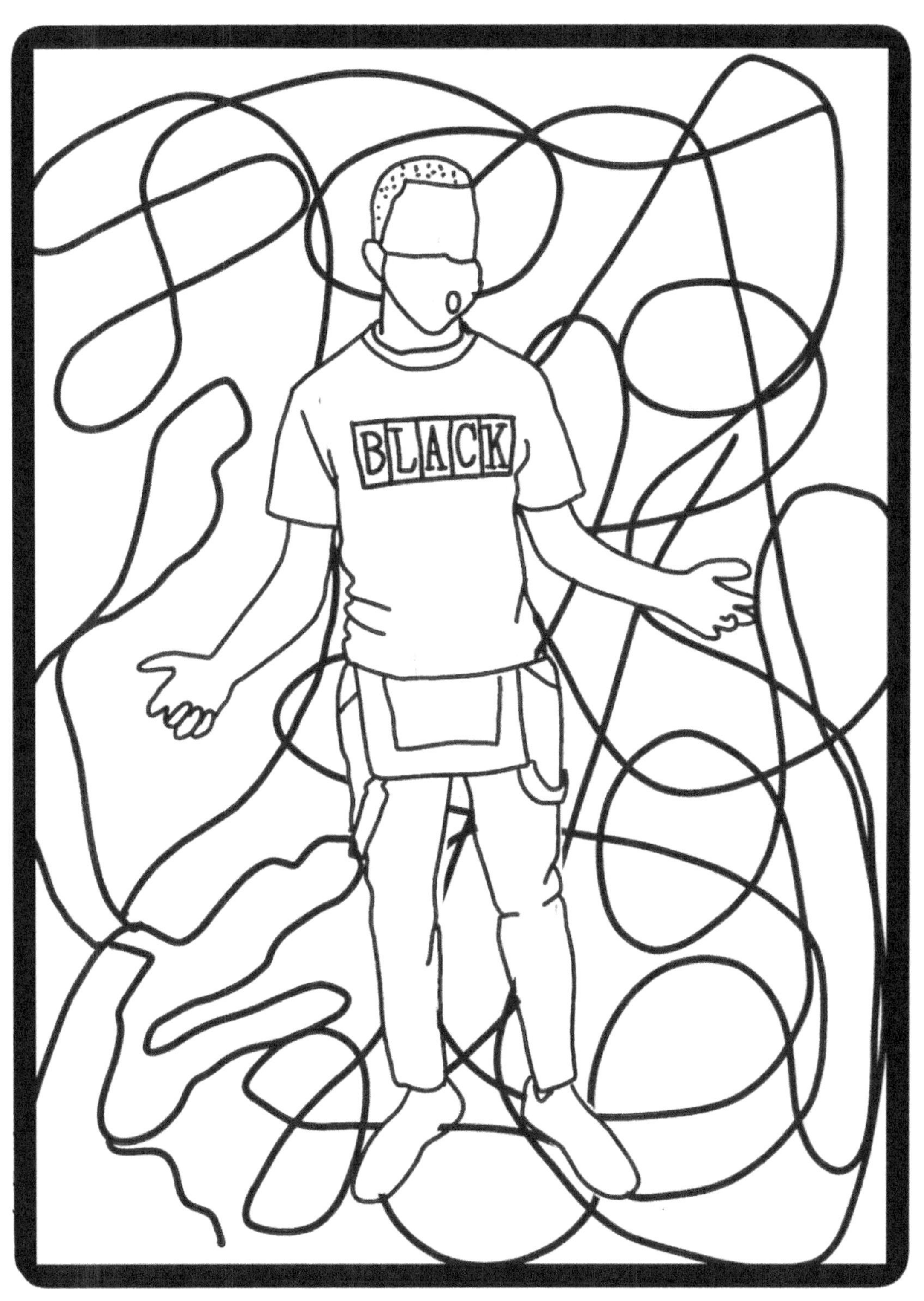
BLACK

Have Pride in Yourself.

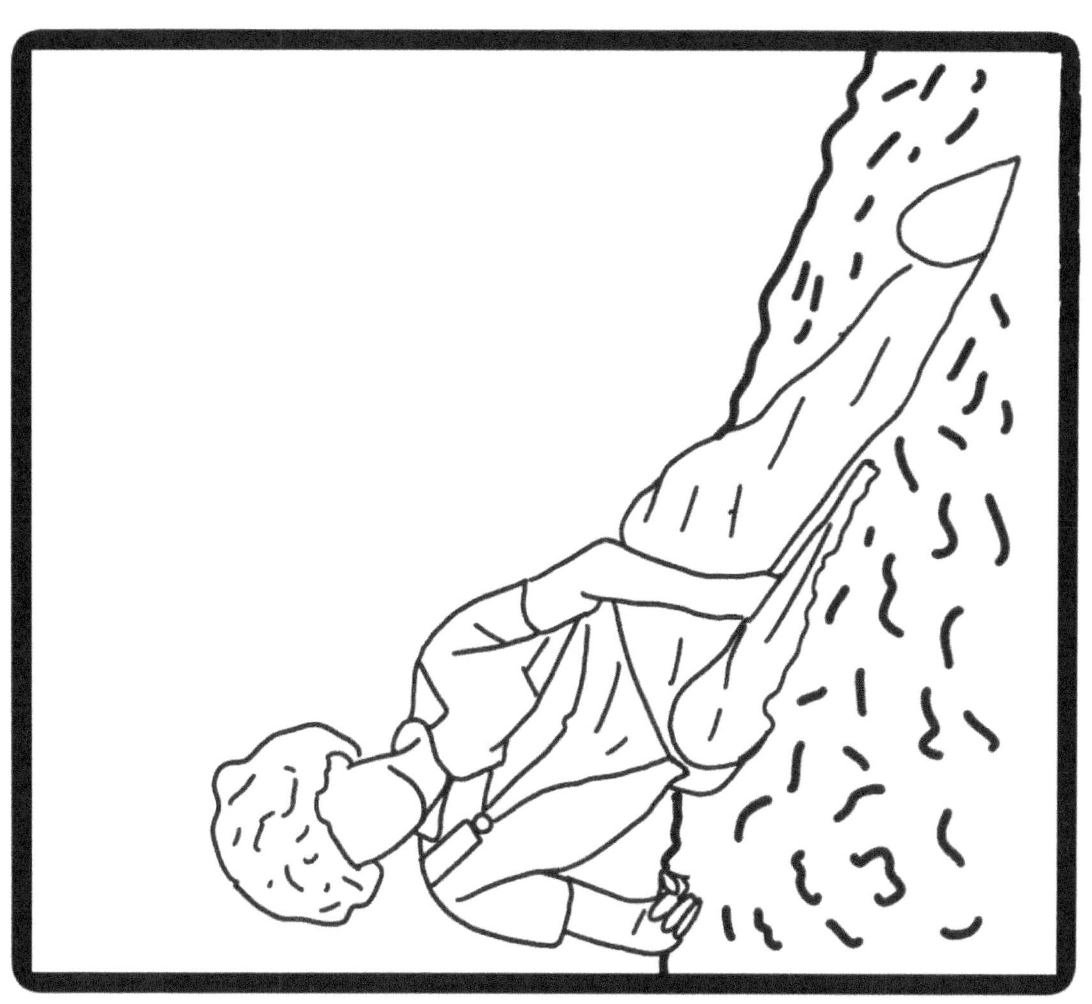

Words of Men Who Laid the Groundwork:

The men included in this section are either historical figures or men who are living, working, through the same struggles that you are. This section was made specifically to let you know that you are not alone in this world. There are men who have done what was necessary to bring about change in the world so you can be where you are now. Be inspired by these men. Take their community activism, their dedication to their movements, and their love of their people as an example for your life.

"Leadership is building a bridge that connects the vision with the purpose, in order to empower those who are around us."

David Walker
Abolitionist/Journalist

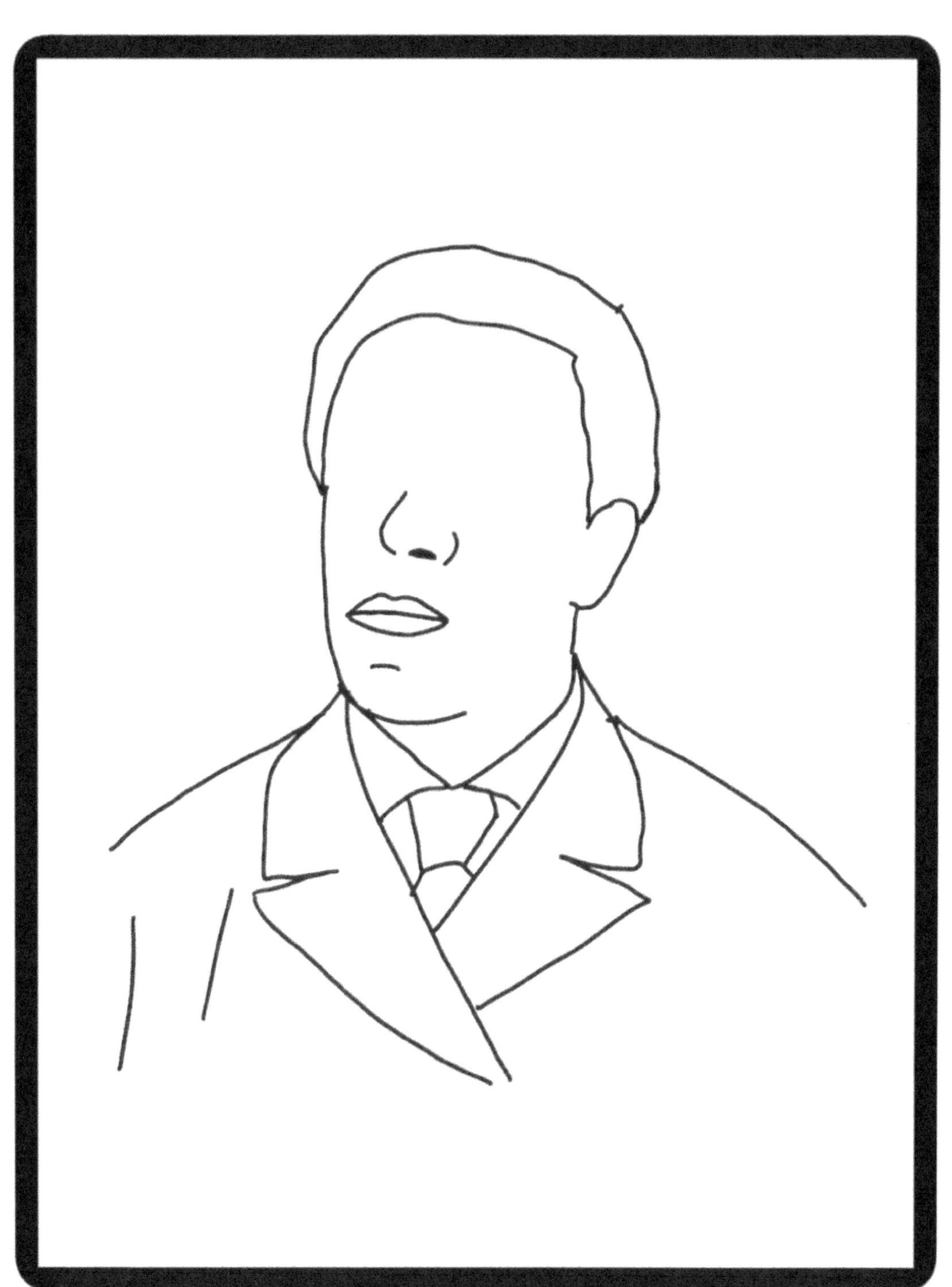

"The answer to injustice is not to silence the critic
but to end the injustice."

Paul Roberson
Musical Artist/Film Actor

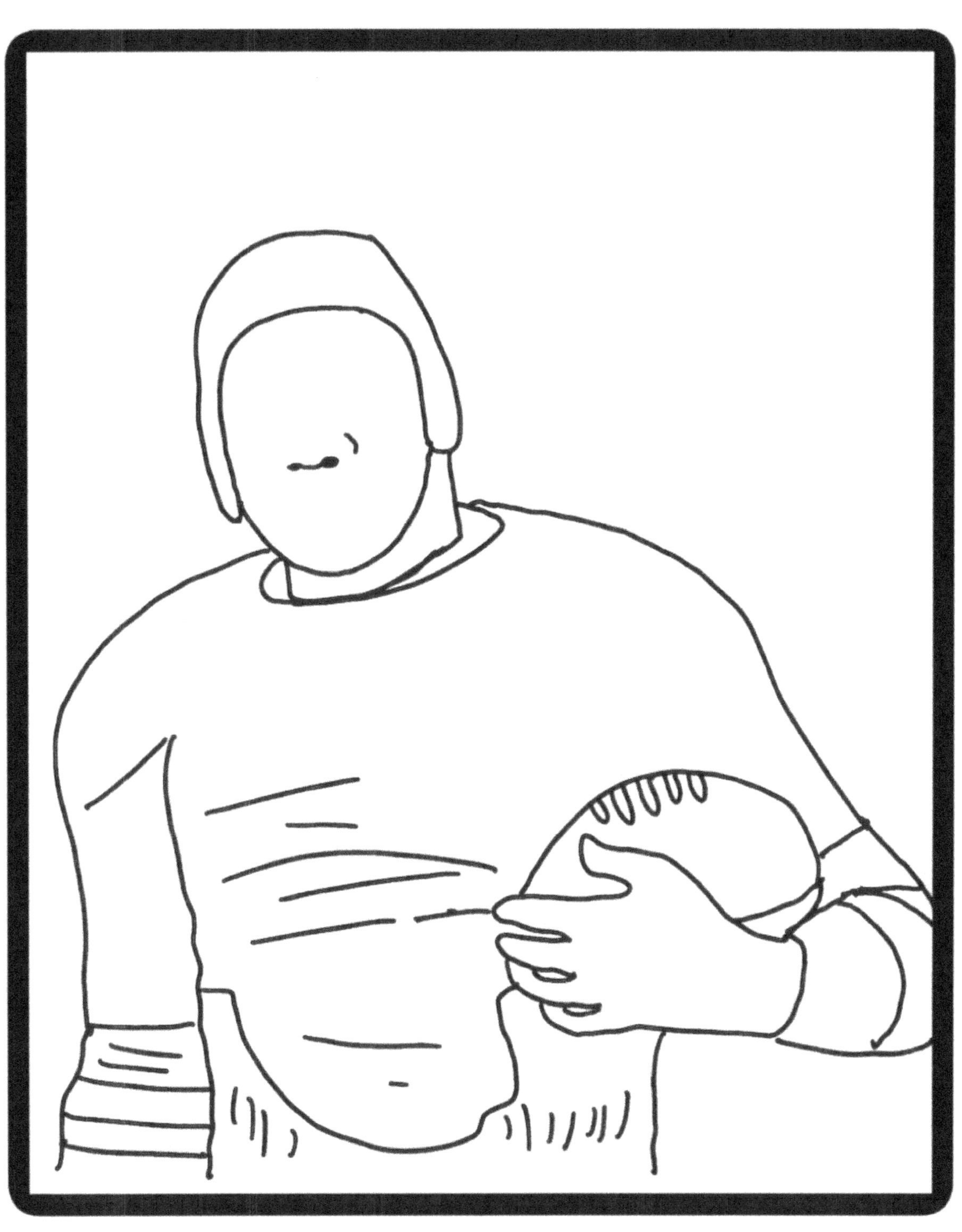

"It's never the right time to take a particular stand."

Adam Clayton Powell Jr.
Pastor/Politician

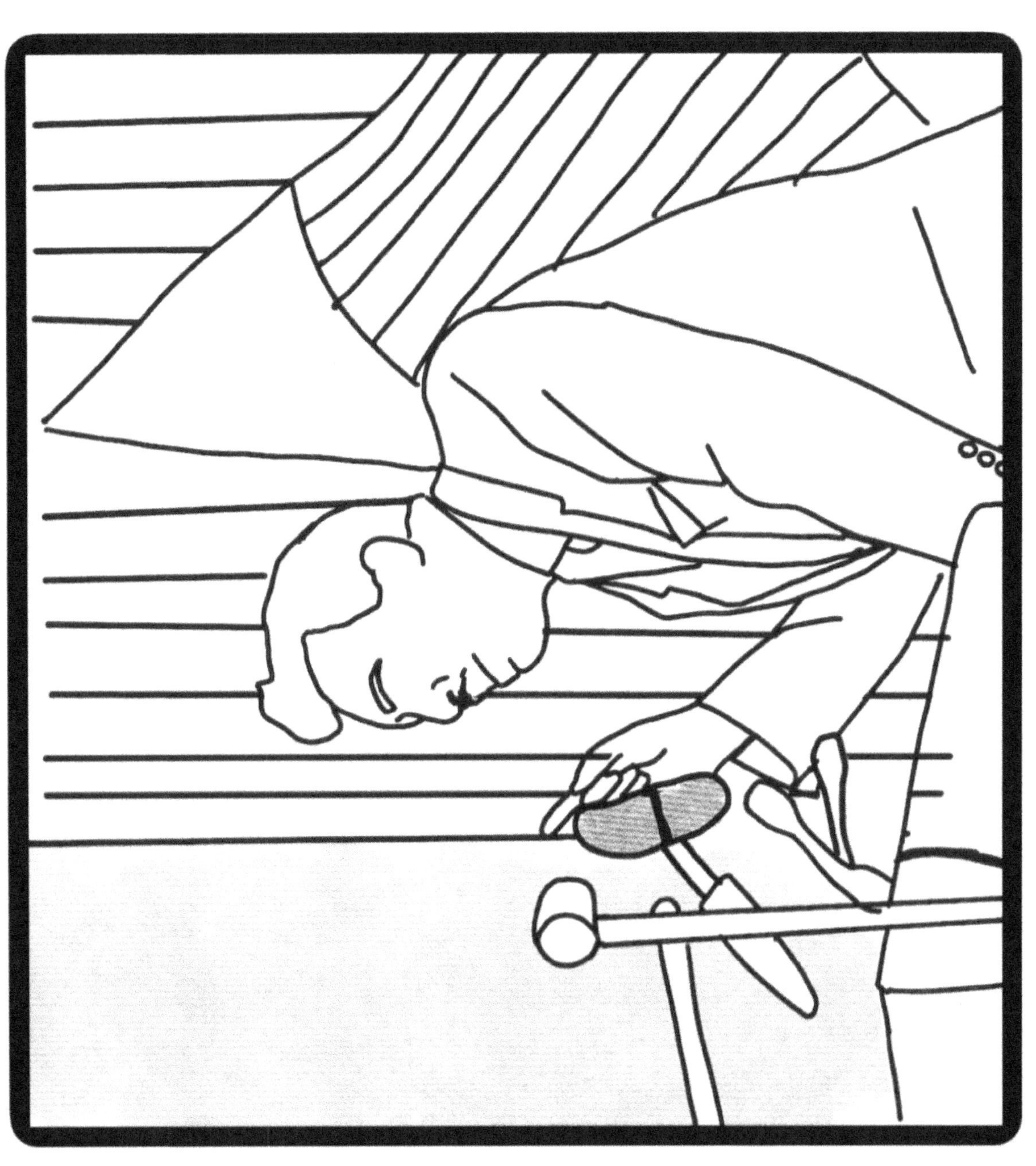

"Love of self comes first. The one who loves
everybody is the one who does not love anyone."

Elijah Muhammad
Leader in the Nation of Islam

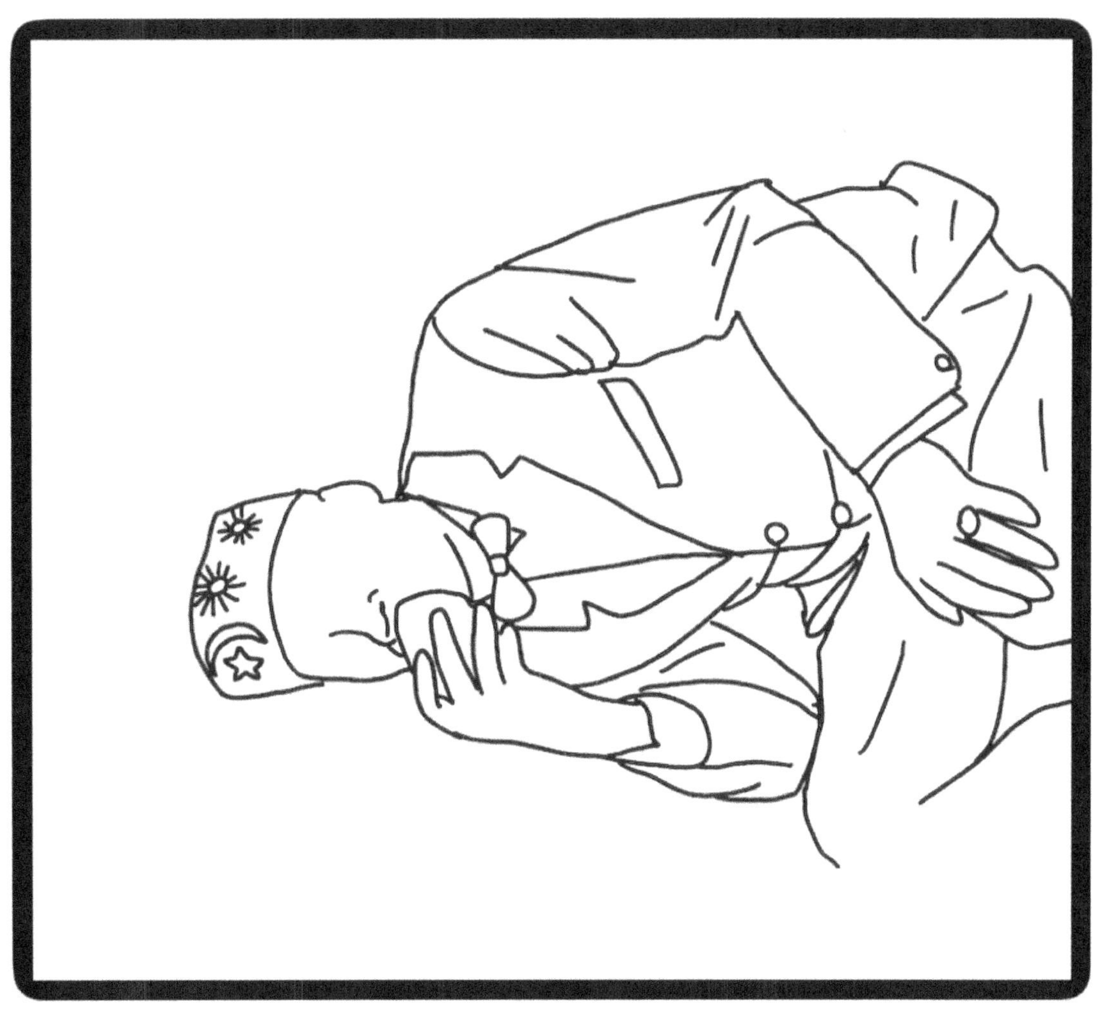

"I have discovered in life that there are ways of getting almost anywhere you want to go if you really want to go."

Langston Hughes
Poet/Novelist/Playwright

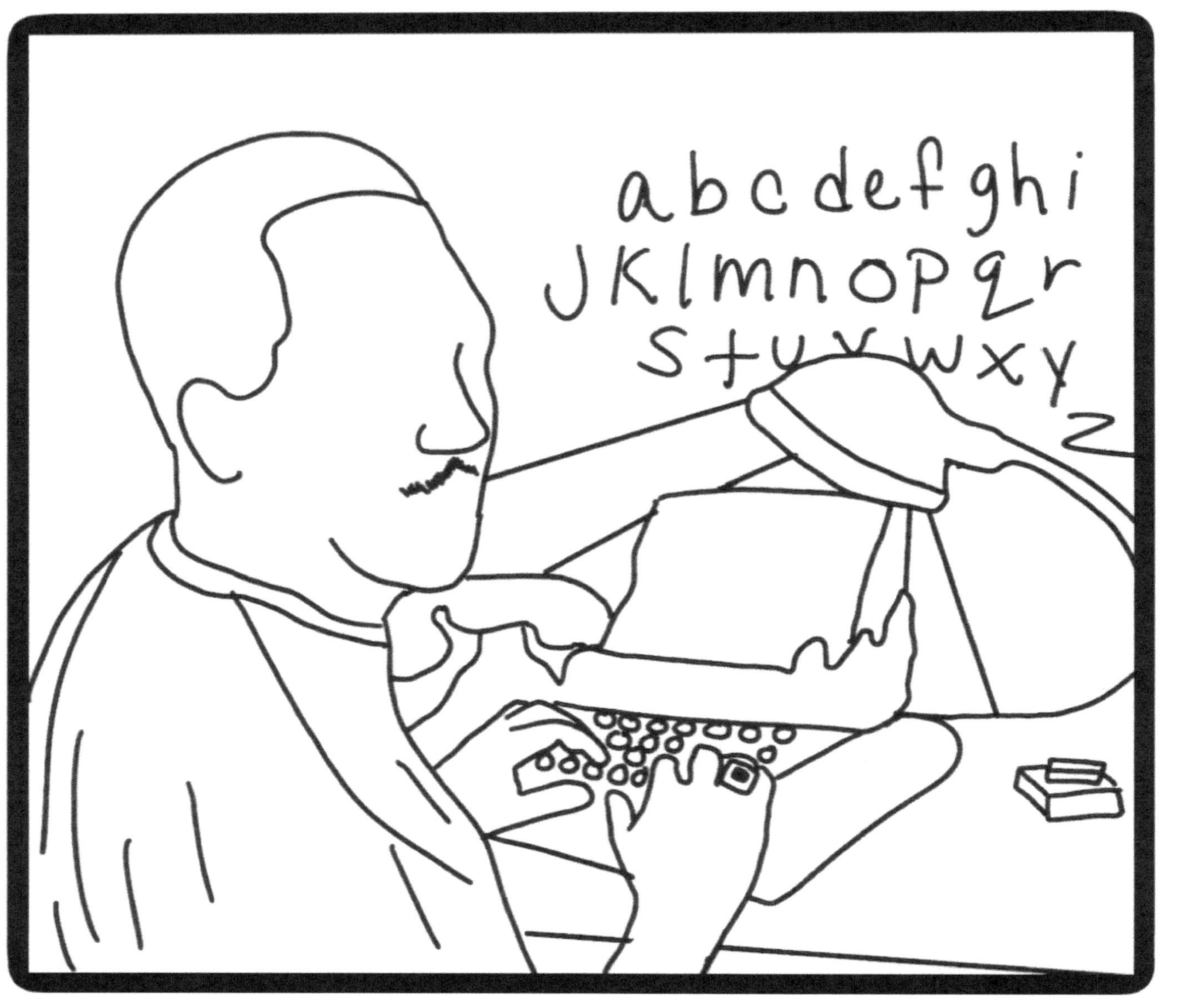

a b c d e f g h i
J K l m n o p q r
s t u v w x y z

"We beg you to save young America from the blight of race prejudice. Do not bind the children within the narrow circles of your own lives."

Charles Houston
Lawyer

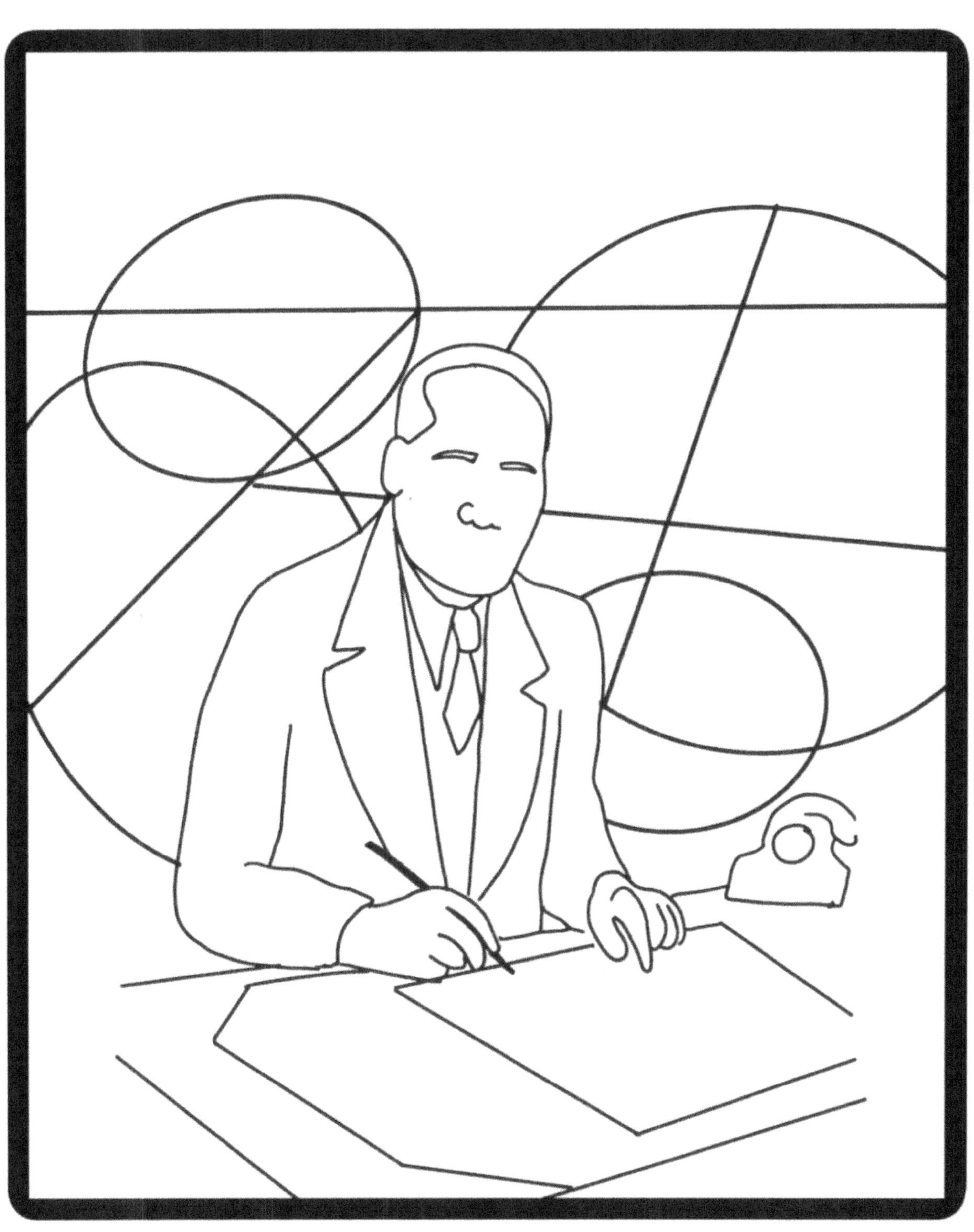

"Go home and tell your daughters they are beautiful."

Kwame Ture
Human Rights Activist

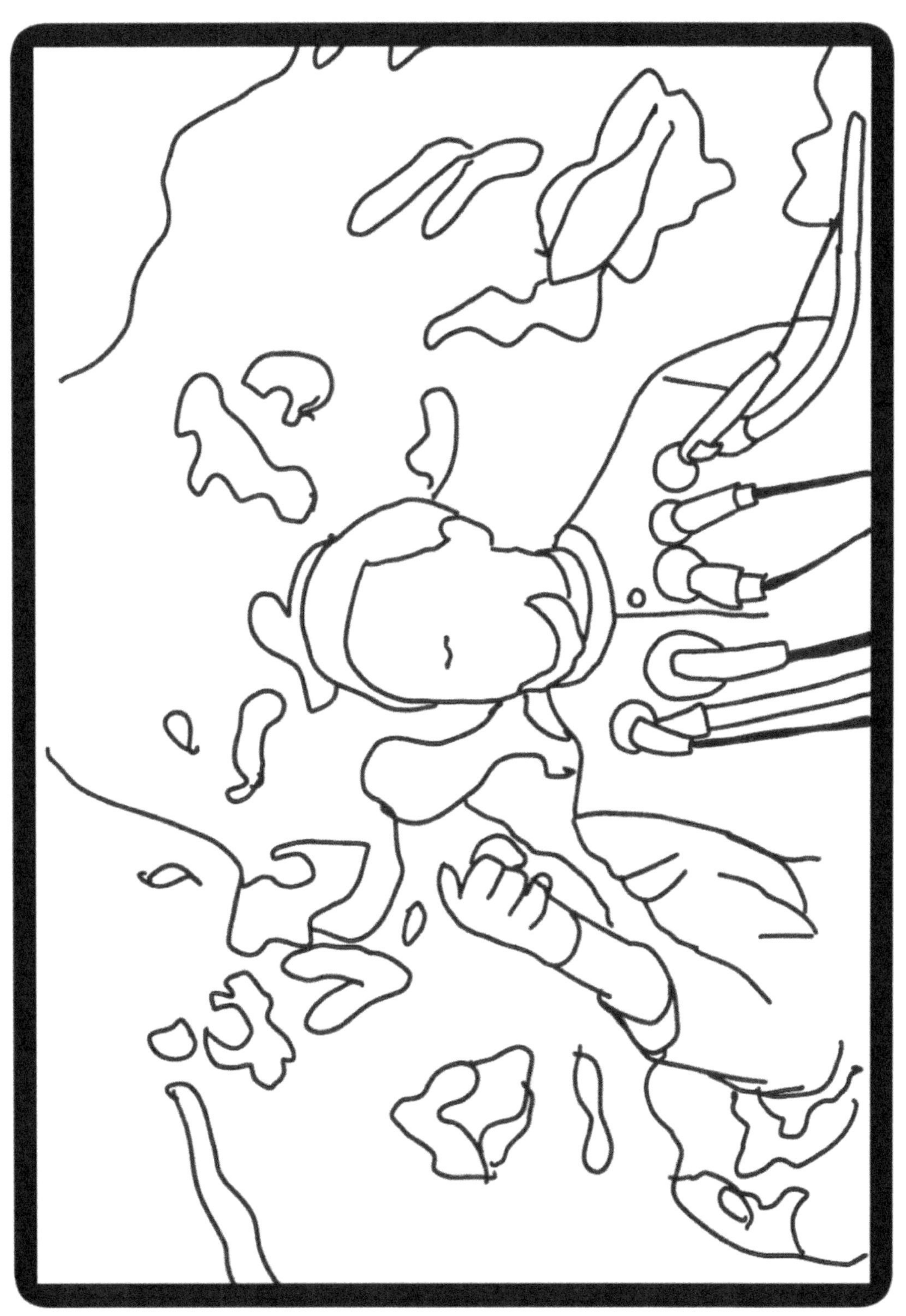

"A problem is a chance for you to do your best."

Duke Ellington
Composer/Pianist

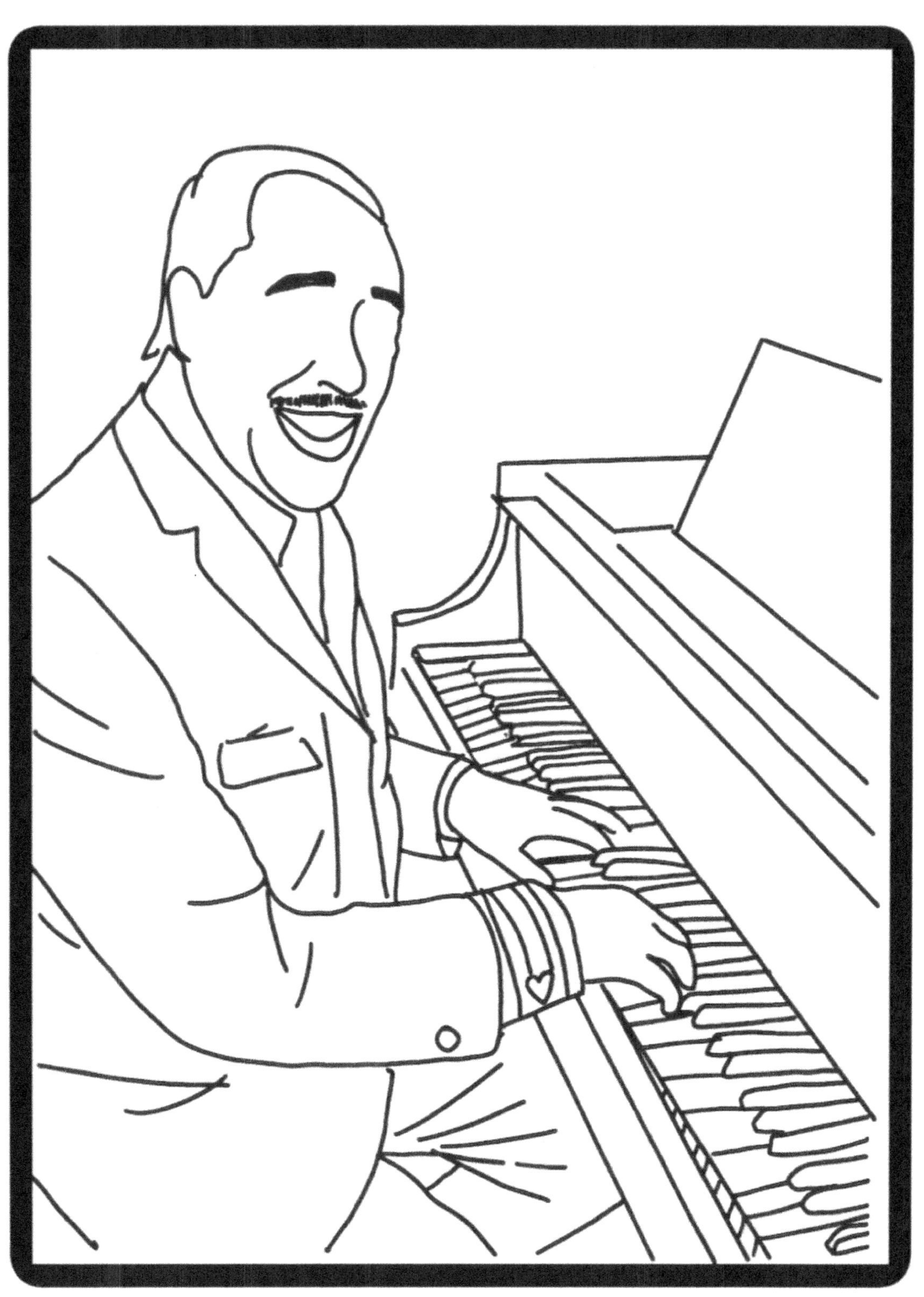

"I've never tried to run away from my race. I was born a black man. You know that in your bones as soon as you are able to understand this country...My approach to life about race is. I don't see the difference between black people and white people."

Edward W. Brooke
First African American U.S. Senator

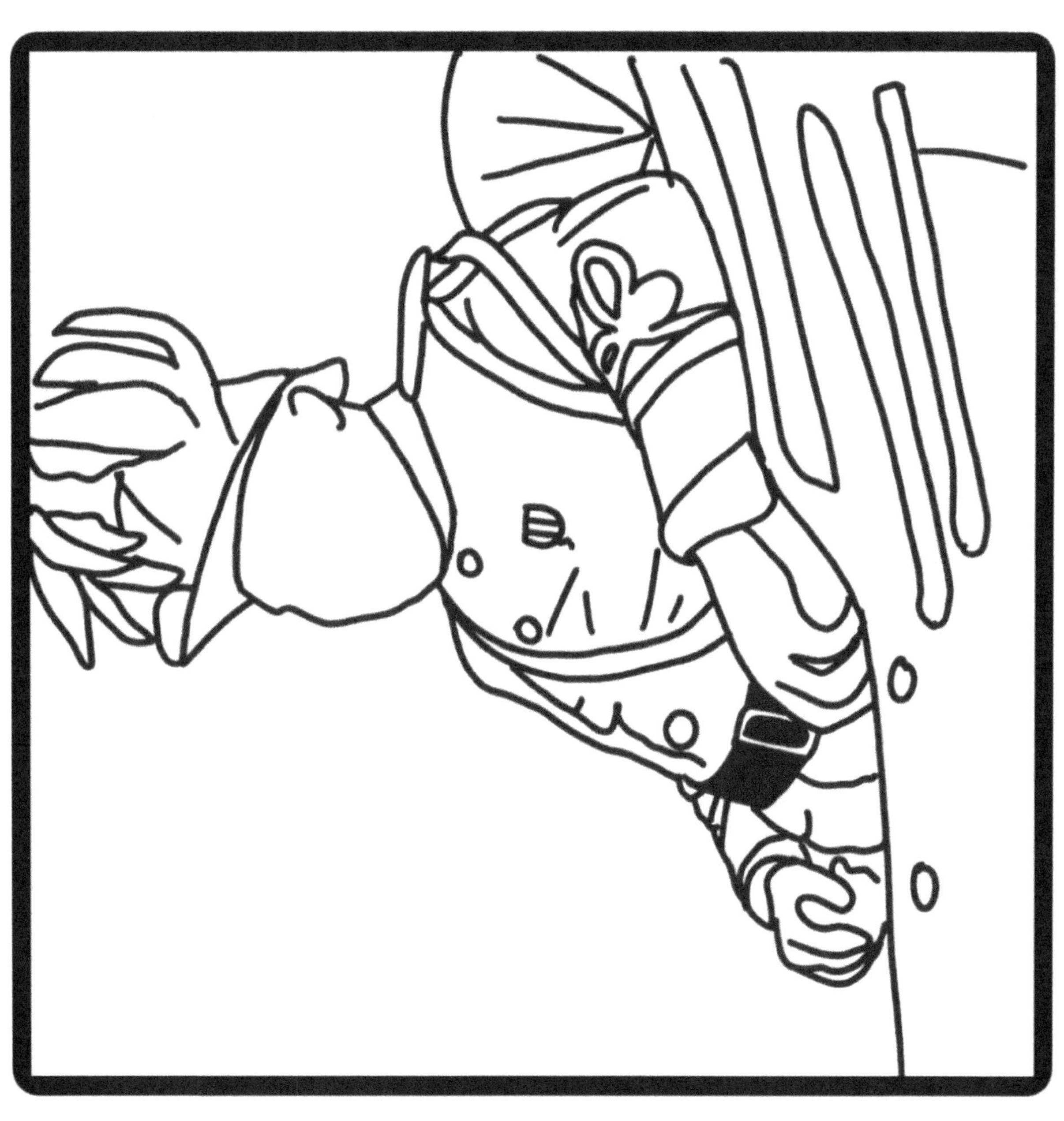

"One ever feels his twoness-an America, A Negro;
two souls; two thoughts; two reconciled strivings;
two earrings ideals in one dark body, whose
dogged strength alone keeps it from being torn
asunder."

WEB Du Bois
Sociologist/Historian/Pan-Africanist

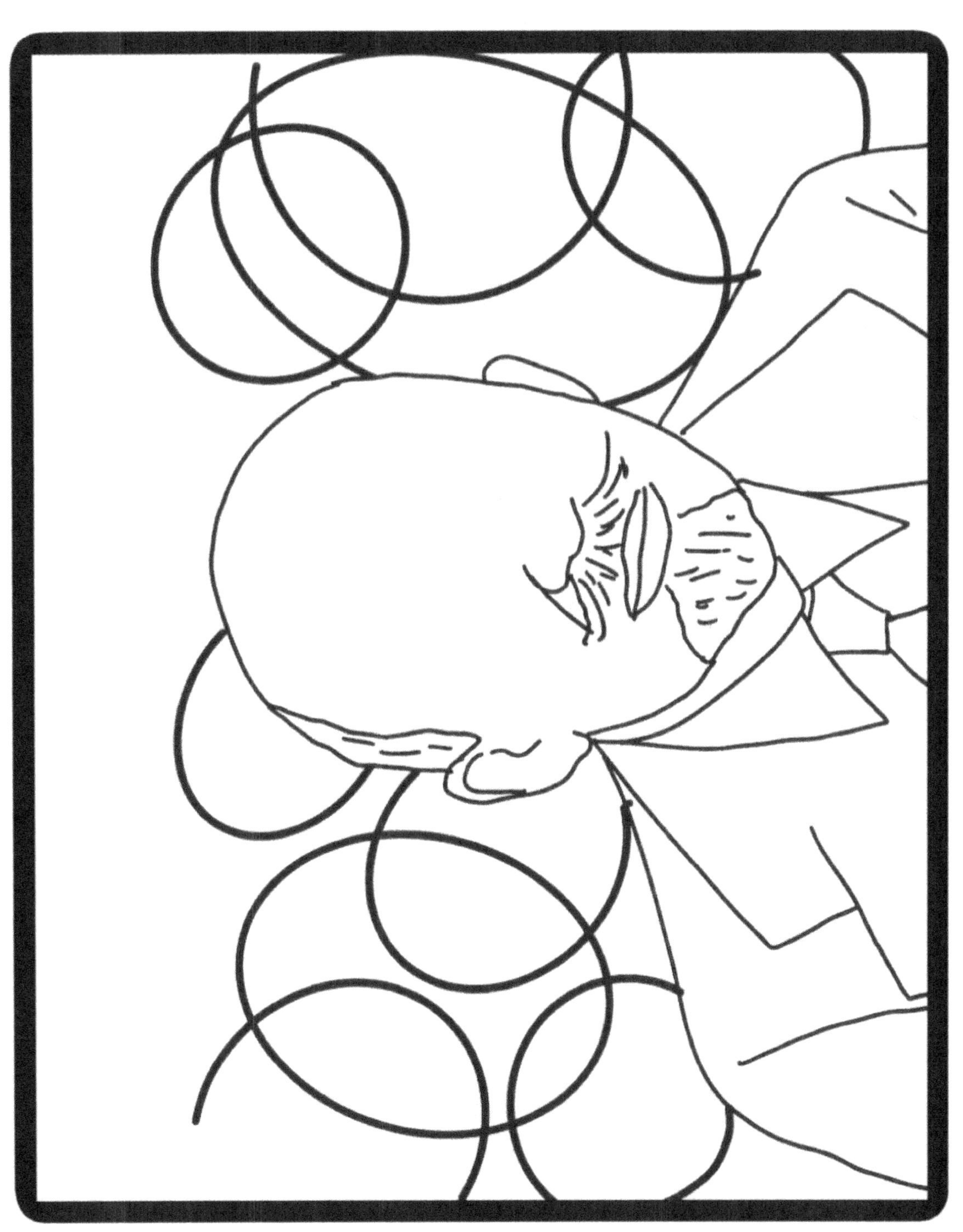

"I've never tried to run away from my race. I was born a black man. You know that in your bones as soon as you are able to understand this country...My approach to life about race is. I don't see the difference between black people and white people."

Edward W. Brooke
First African American U.S. Senator

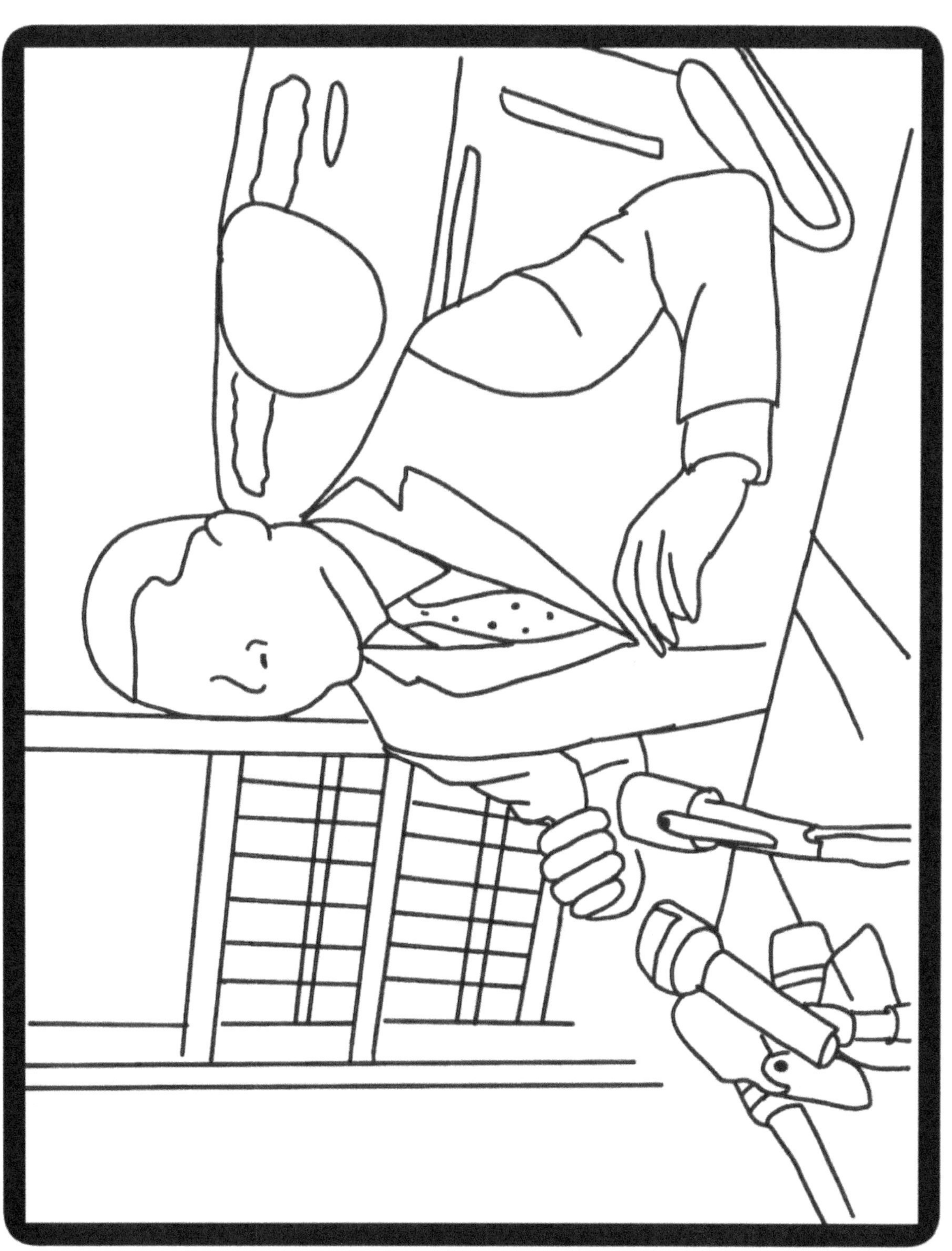

"We have a responsibility to carry the fire, be it in our stomachs or on the end of torches."

Amiri Baraka
Poet/Author

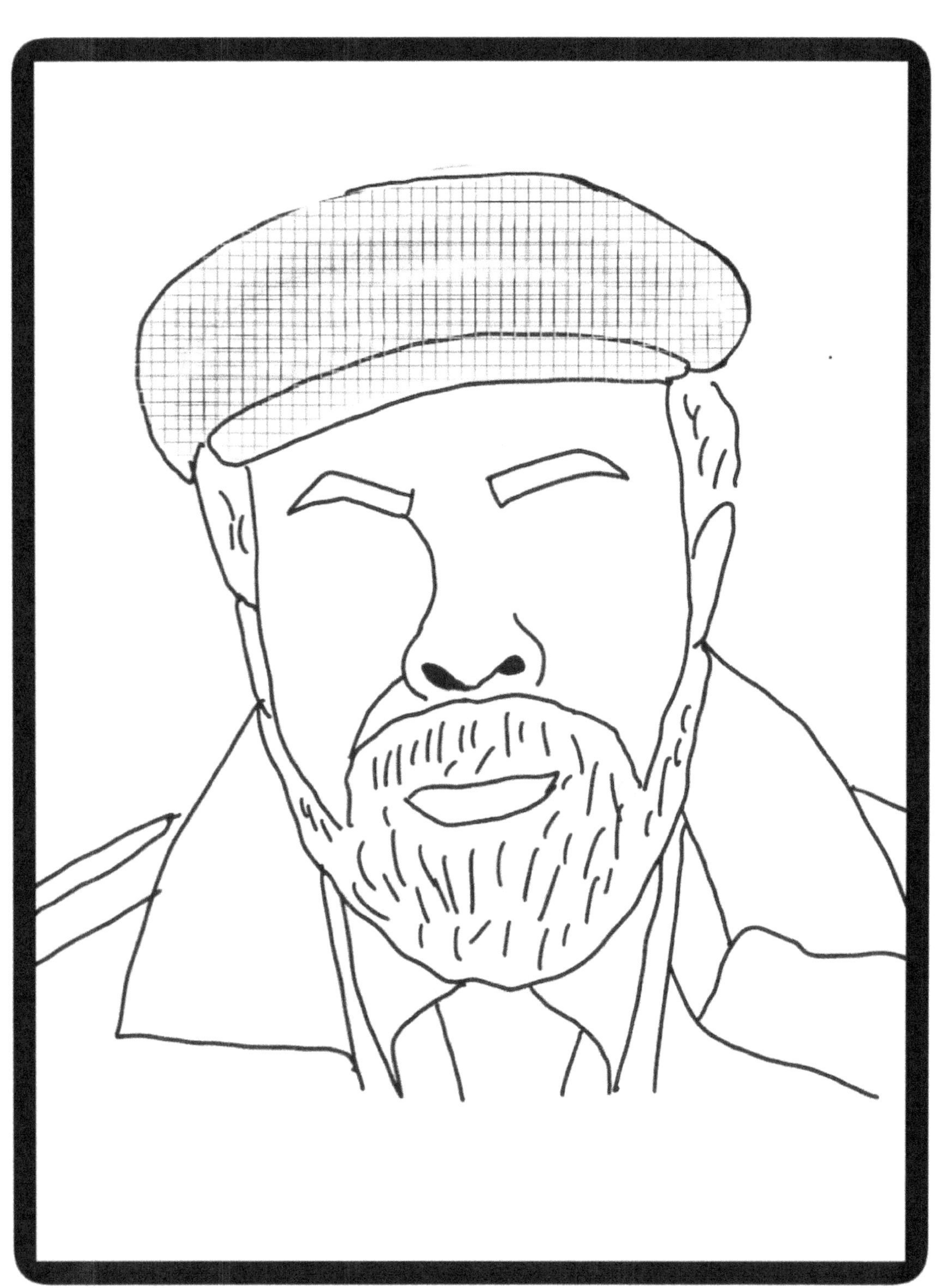

"No greater glory, no greater honor, is the lot of man departing than a feeling possessed deep in his heart that the world is a better place for his having lived."

Robert Abbott
Artist/Illustrator

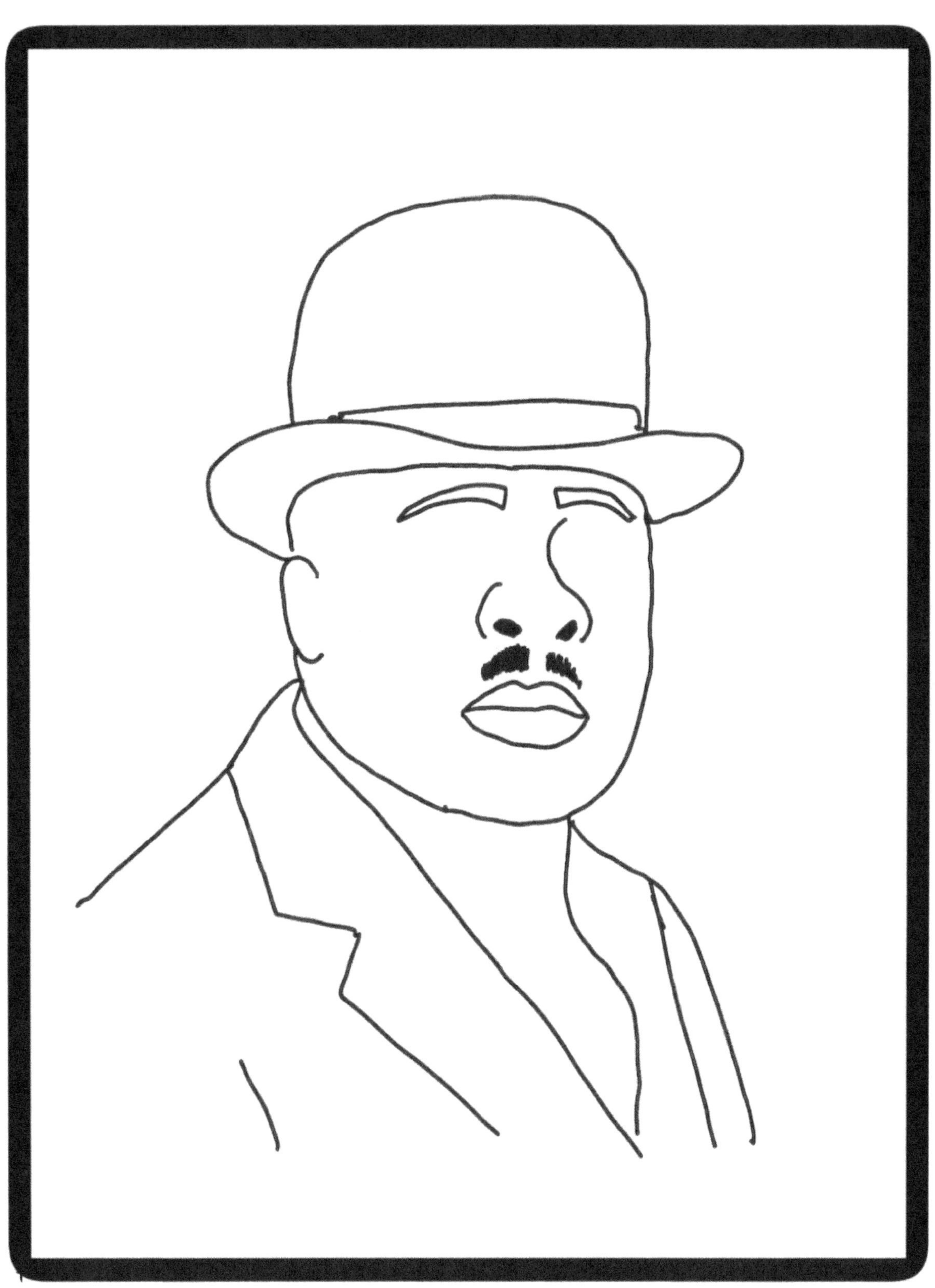

"You can't hold a man down without staying down with him"

Booker T. Washington
Educator/Author-American Civil Rights Leader

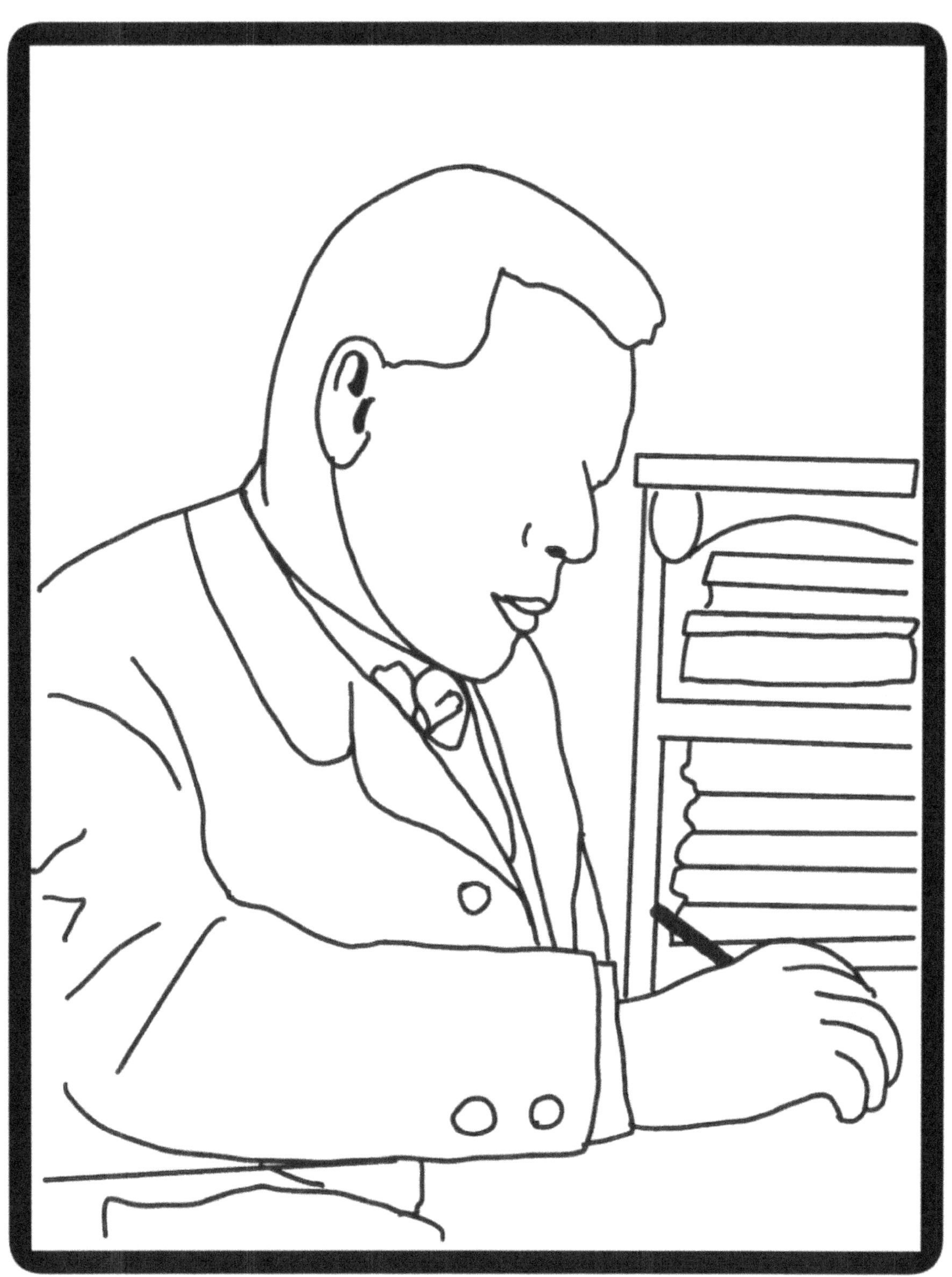

"It is easier to build strong children than to repair broken men."

Frederick Douglas
Abolitionist/Writer/Social Reformer

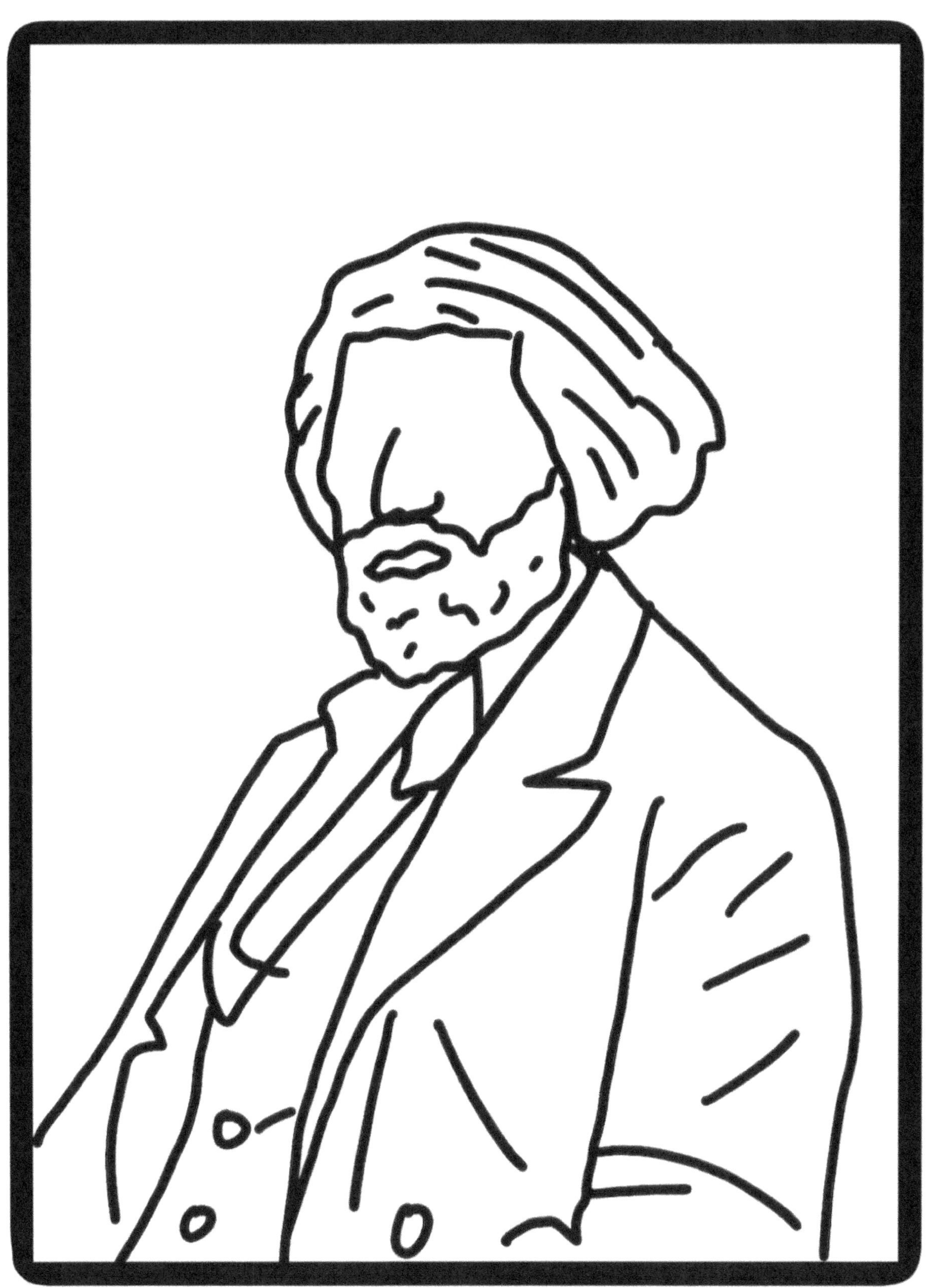

"If my mind can conceive it and my heart can
believe it--then I can achieve it."

Muhammad Ali
Award-winning boxer

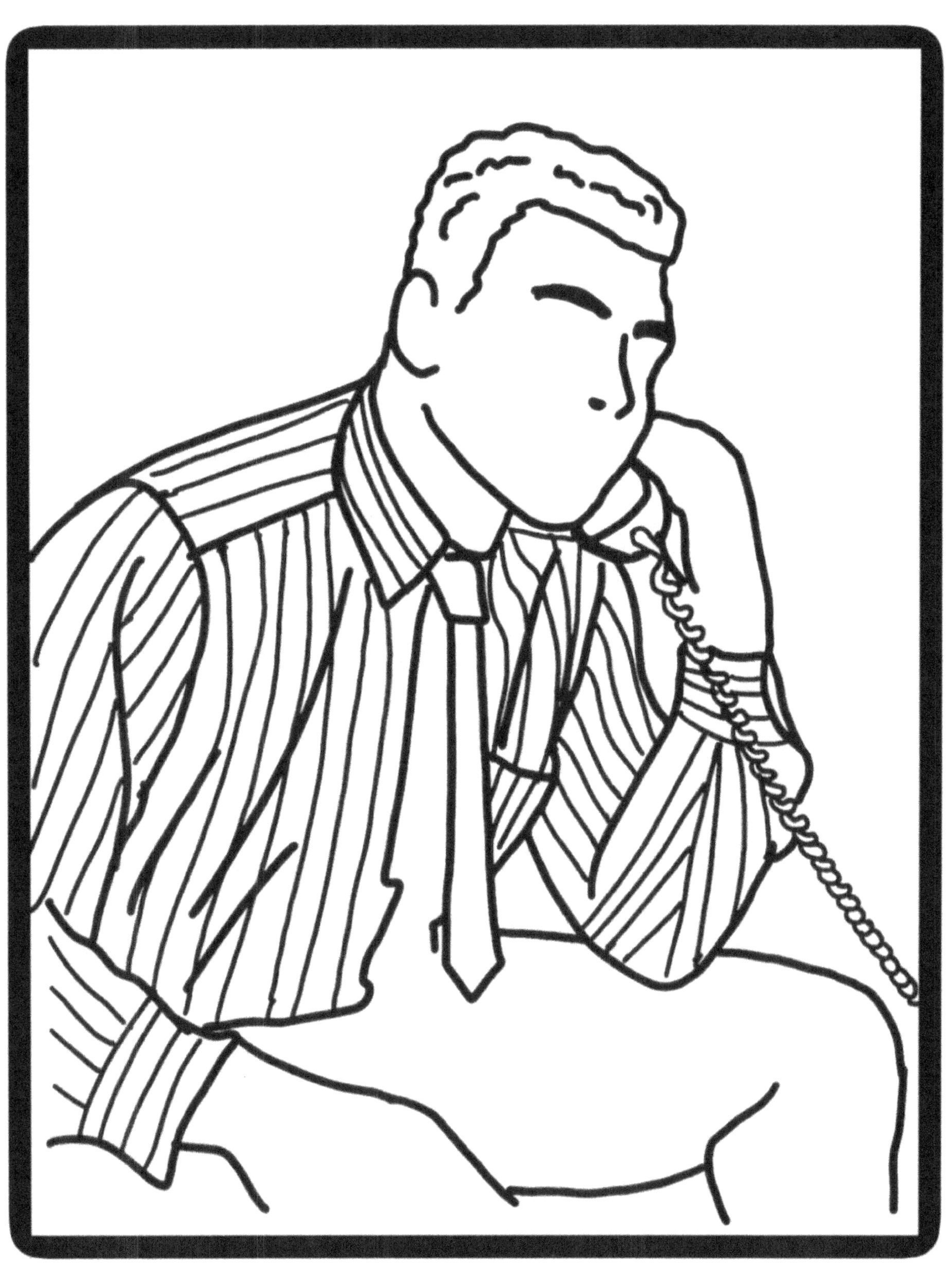

"None of us are hot where we are solely by
pulling ourselves up by our bootstrap. We got here
because somebody bent down and helped us pick
up our boots."

Thurgood Marshalls
Associate Justice of the U.S. Supreme Court

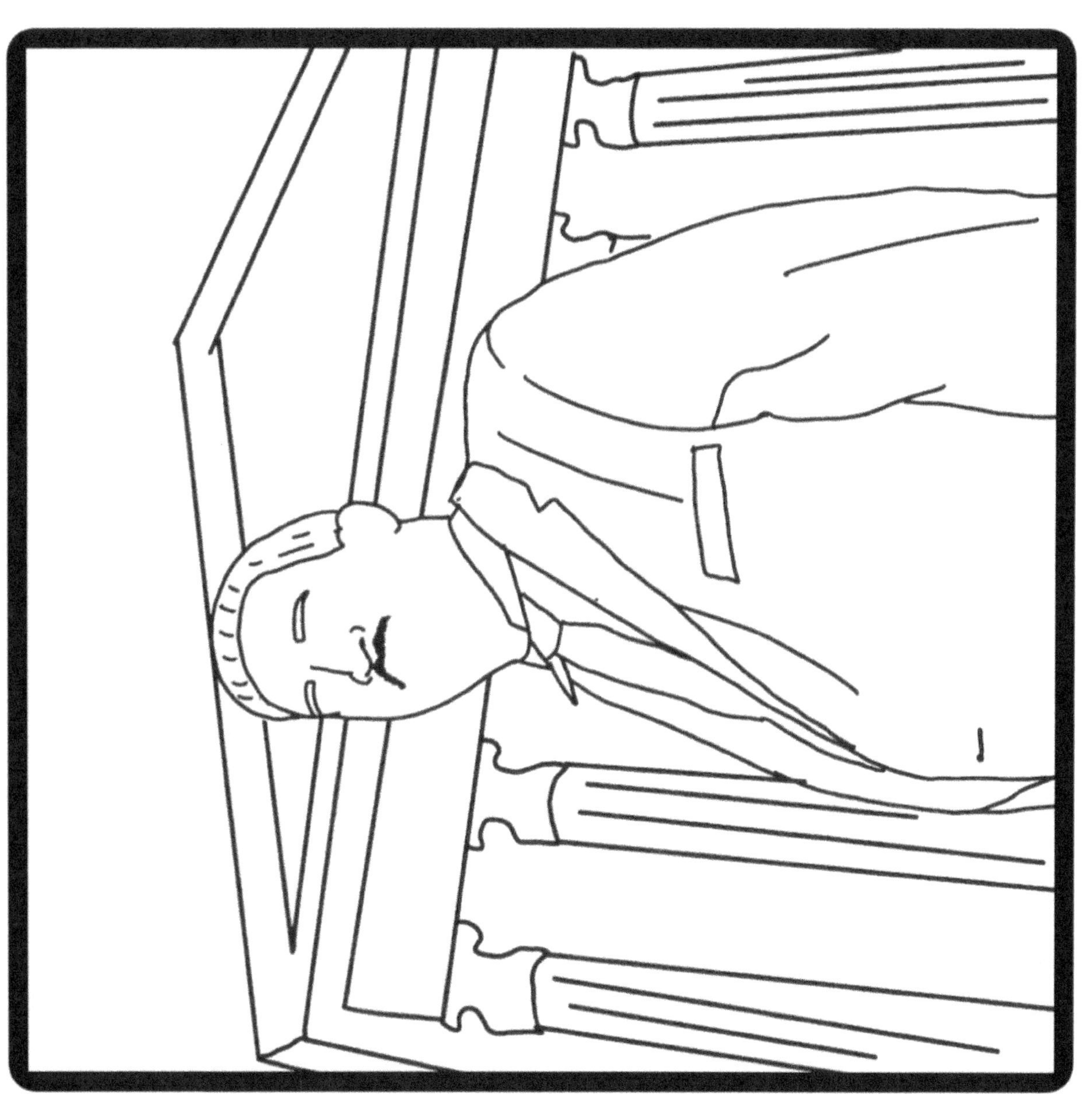

"As we let our light shine, we unconsciously give
other people permission to do so."

Nelson Mandela
South African anti-apartheid revolutionary

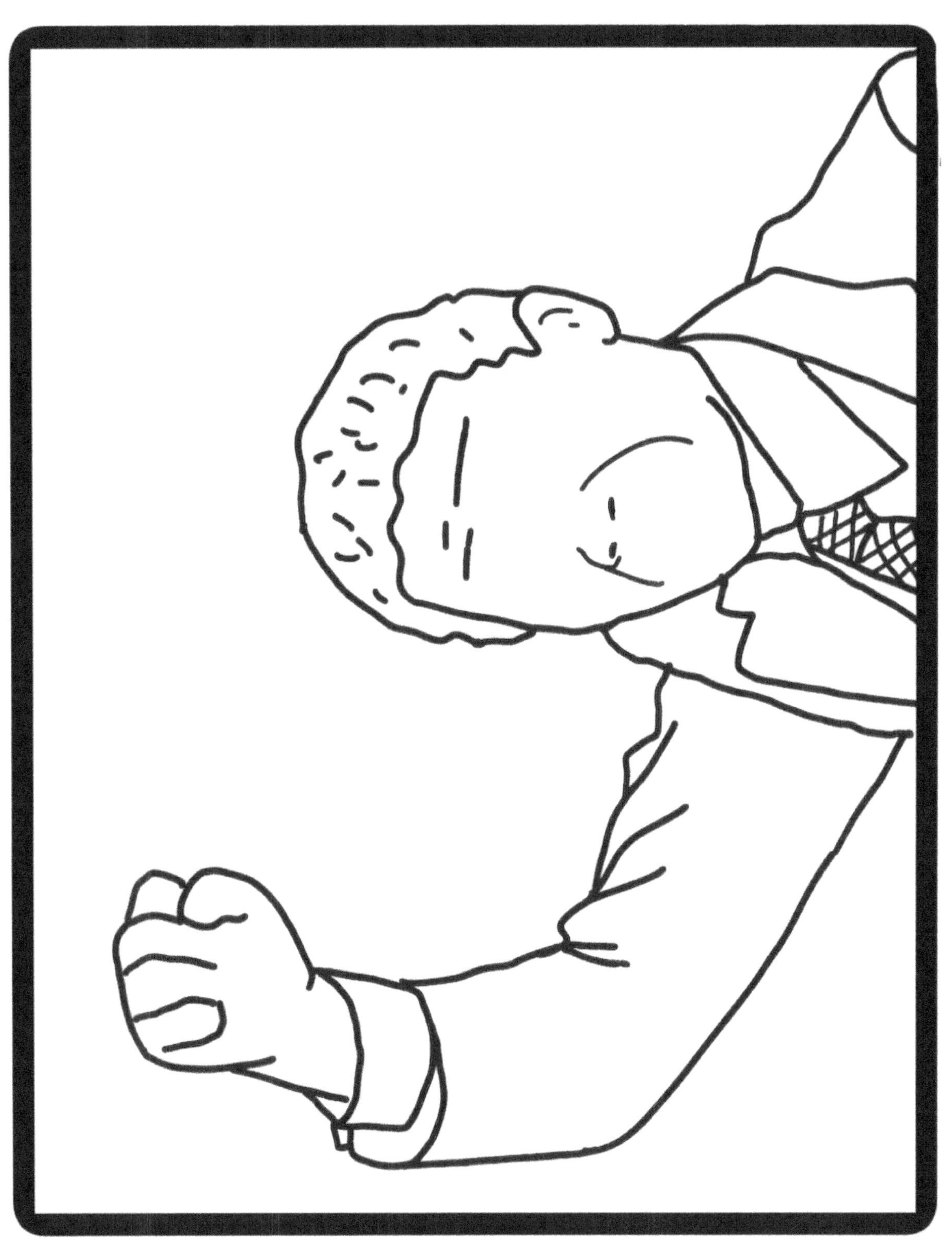

"No matter who you are or what you look like,
how you started off, or how and who you love,
America is a place where you can write your own
destiny."

Barack Obama
44th President of the United States

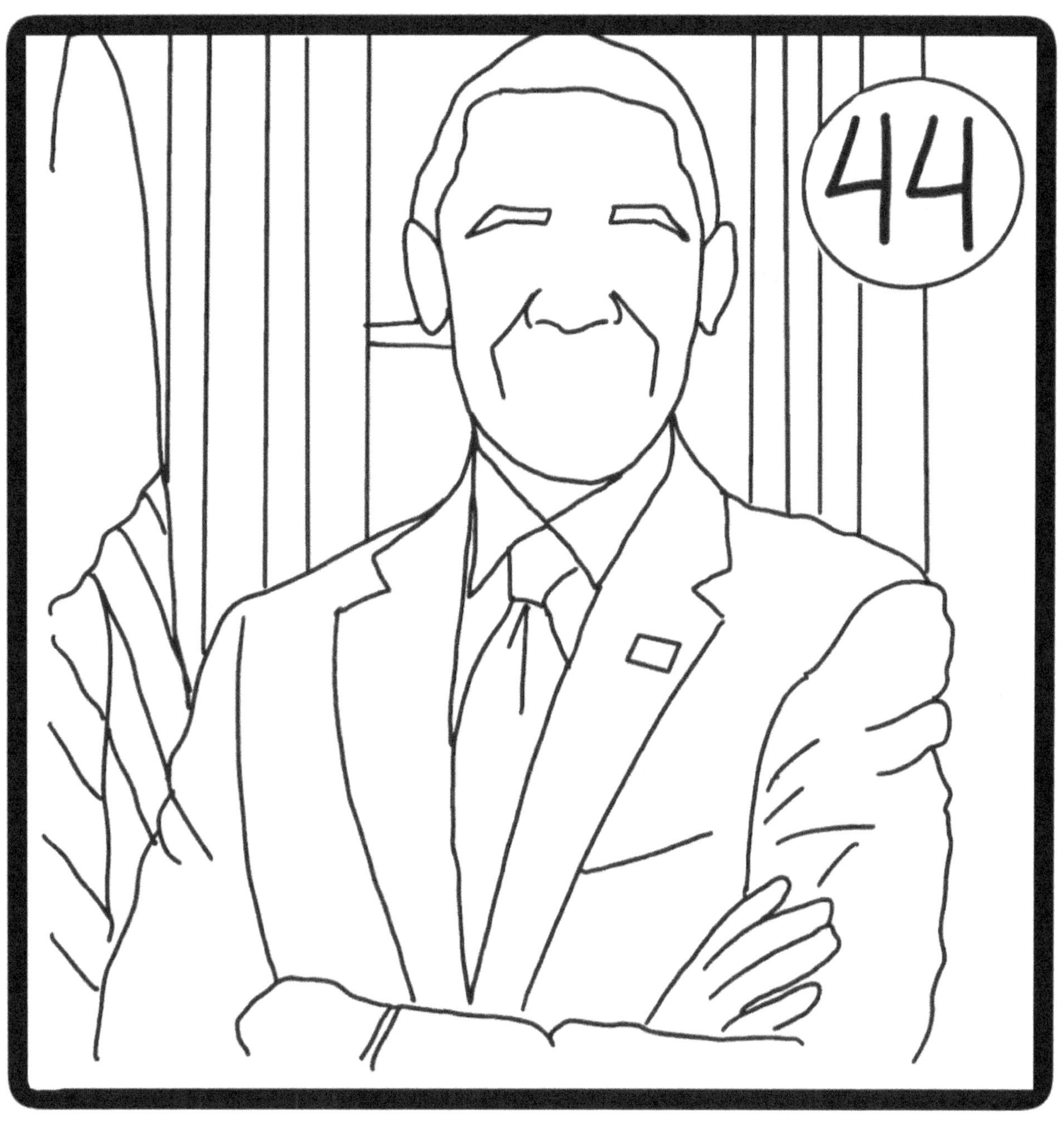

44

"We black folks, our history, and our present being are a mirror of all the manifold experiences of America. What we want, what we represent, what we endure is what America is. If we black folk perish, America will perish."

Richard Wright
Novelist/Poet

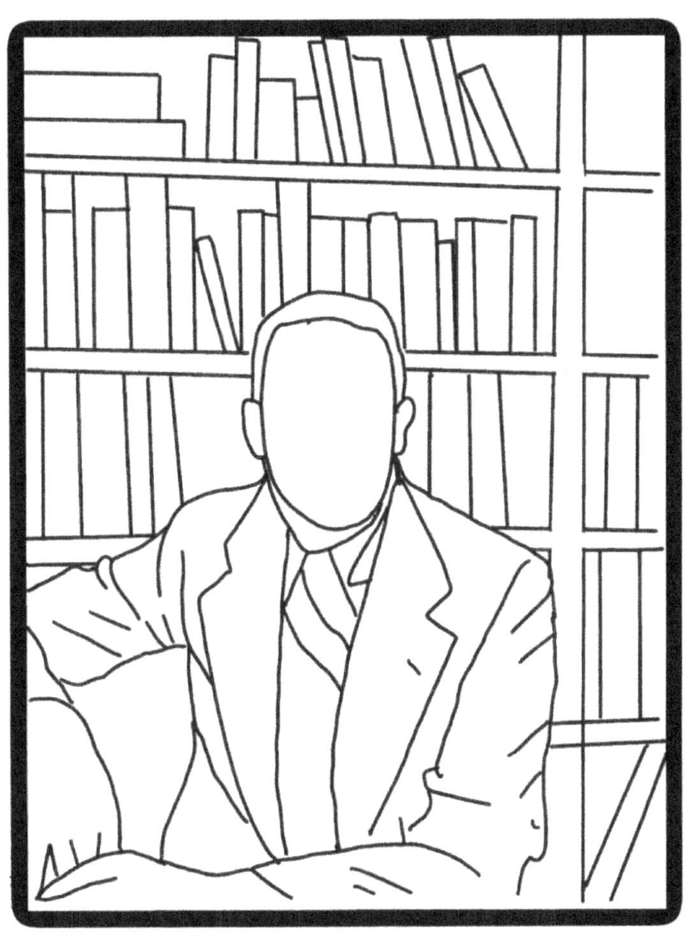

"No man knows what he can do until he tries."

Carter G. Woodson
Historian/Journalist/Author

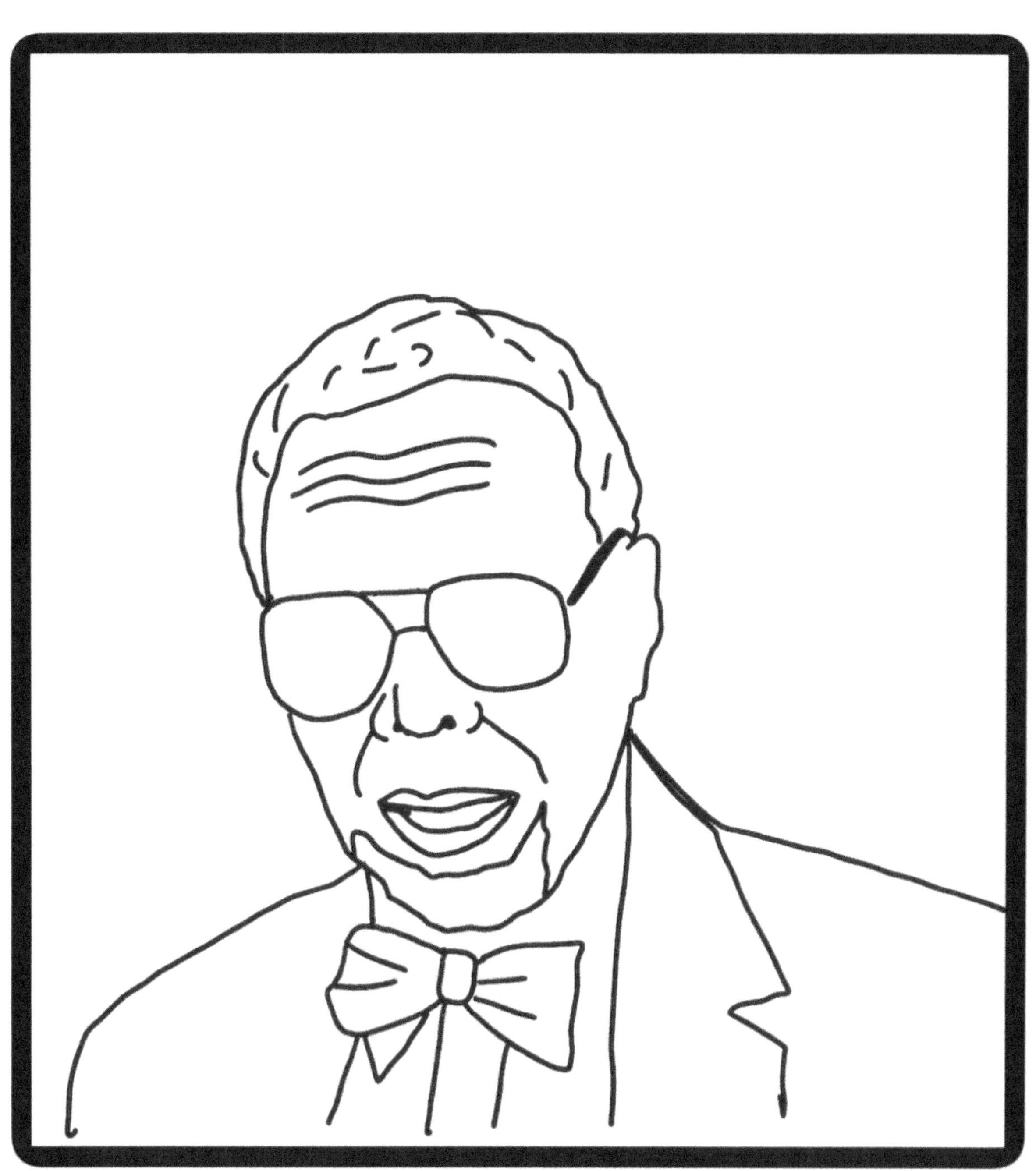

"Confront the dark parts of yourself, and work to banish them with illumination and forgiveness. Your willingness to wrestle with your demons will cause your angels to sing."

August Wilson
Author/Playwright

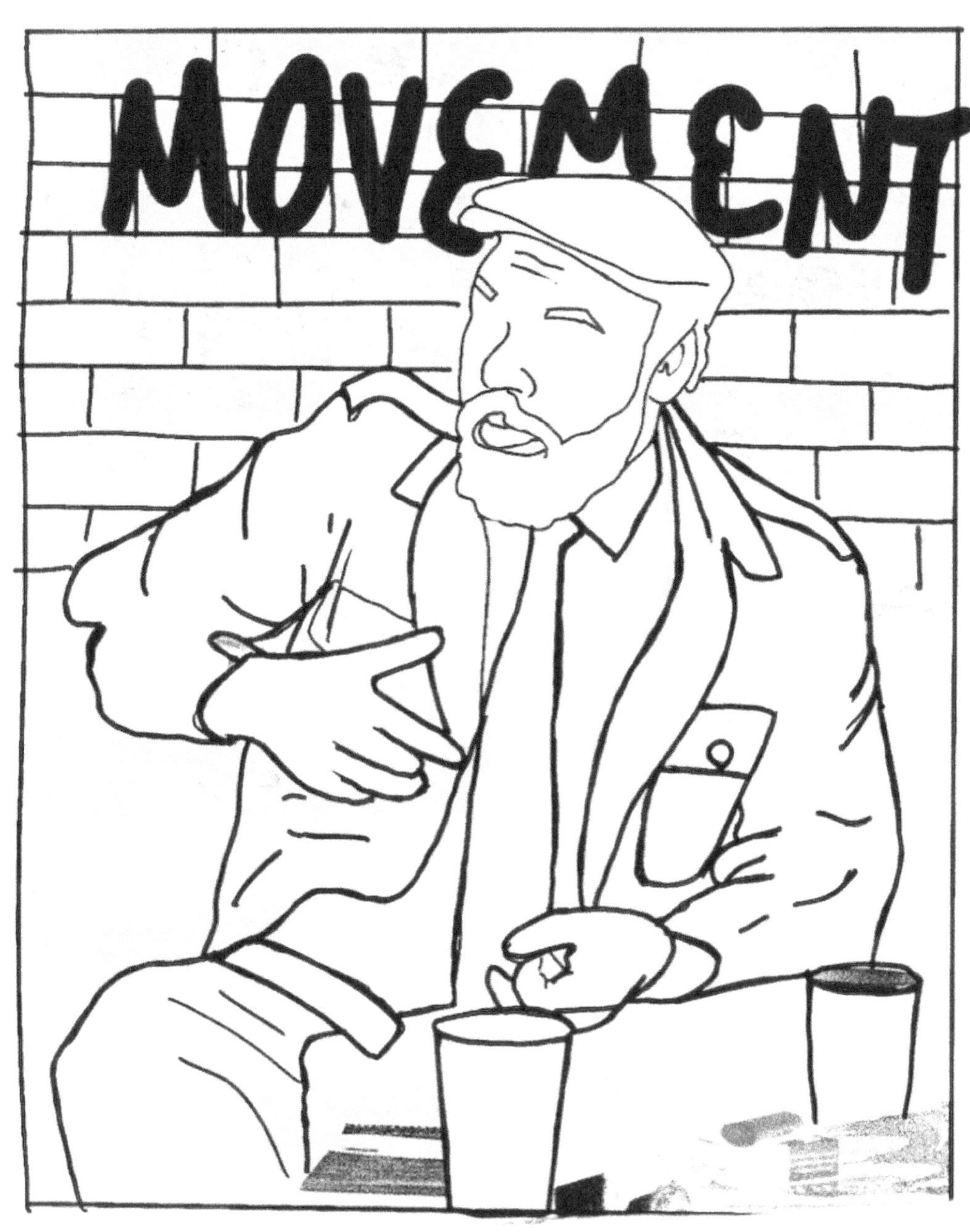
MOVEMENT

"Injustice anywhere is a threat to justice everywhere."

Martin Luther King Jr.
Minister/Civil Rights Leader

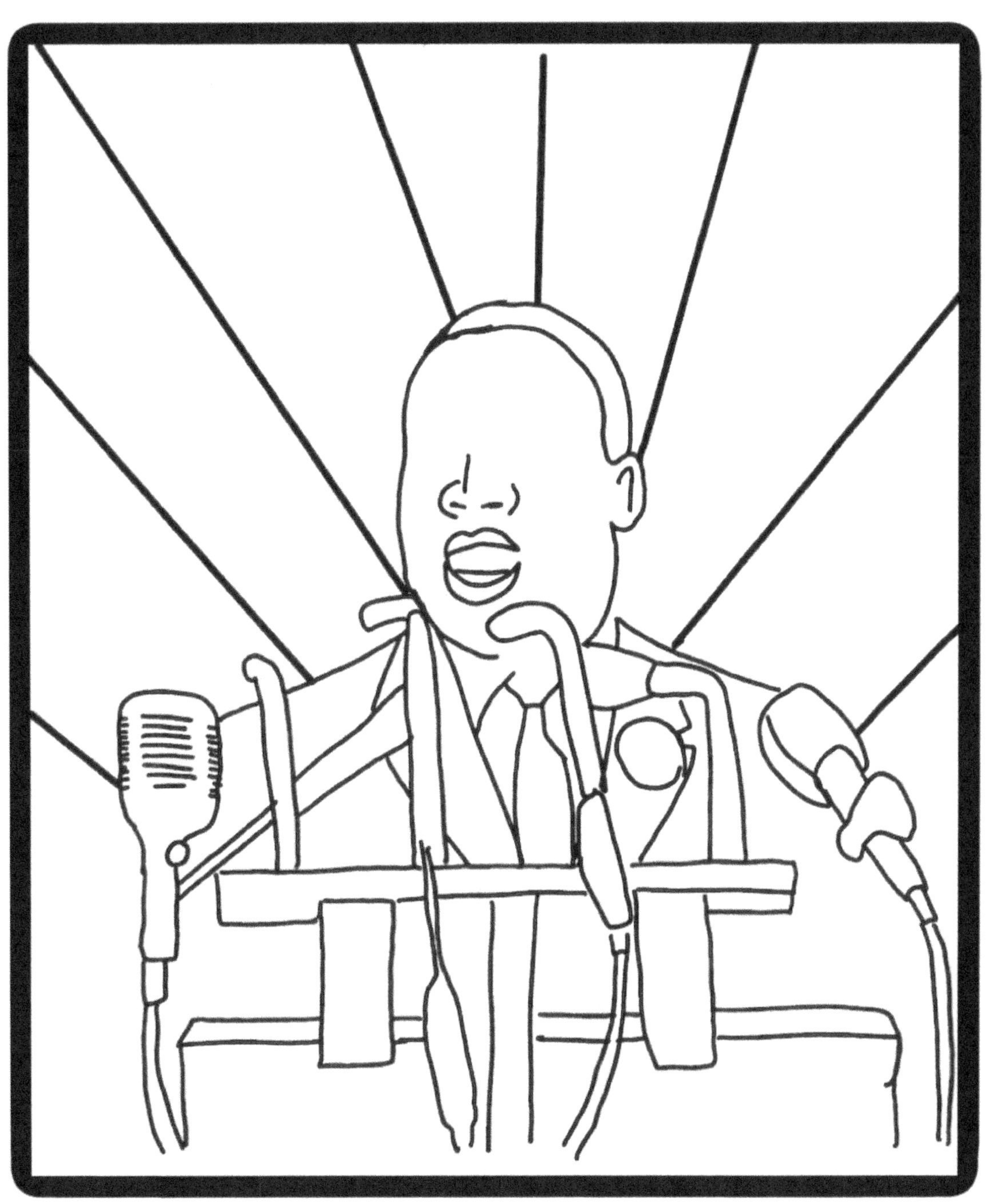

"A man who stands for nothing will fall for
anything."

Malcolm X
Minister/Human Rights Activist

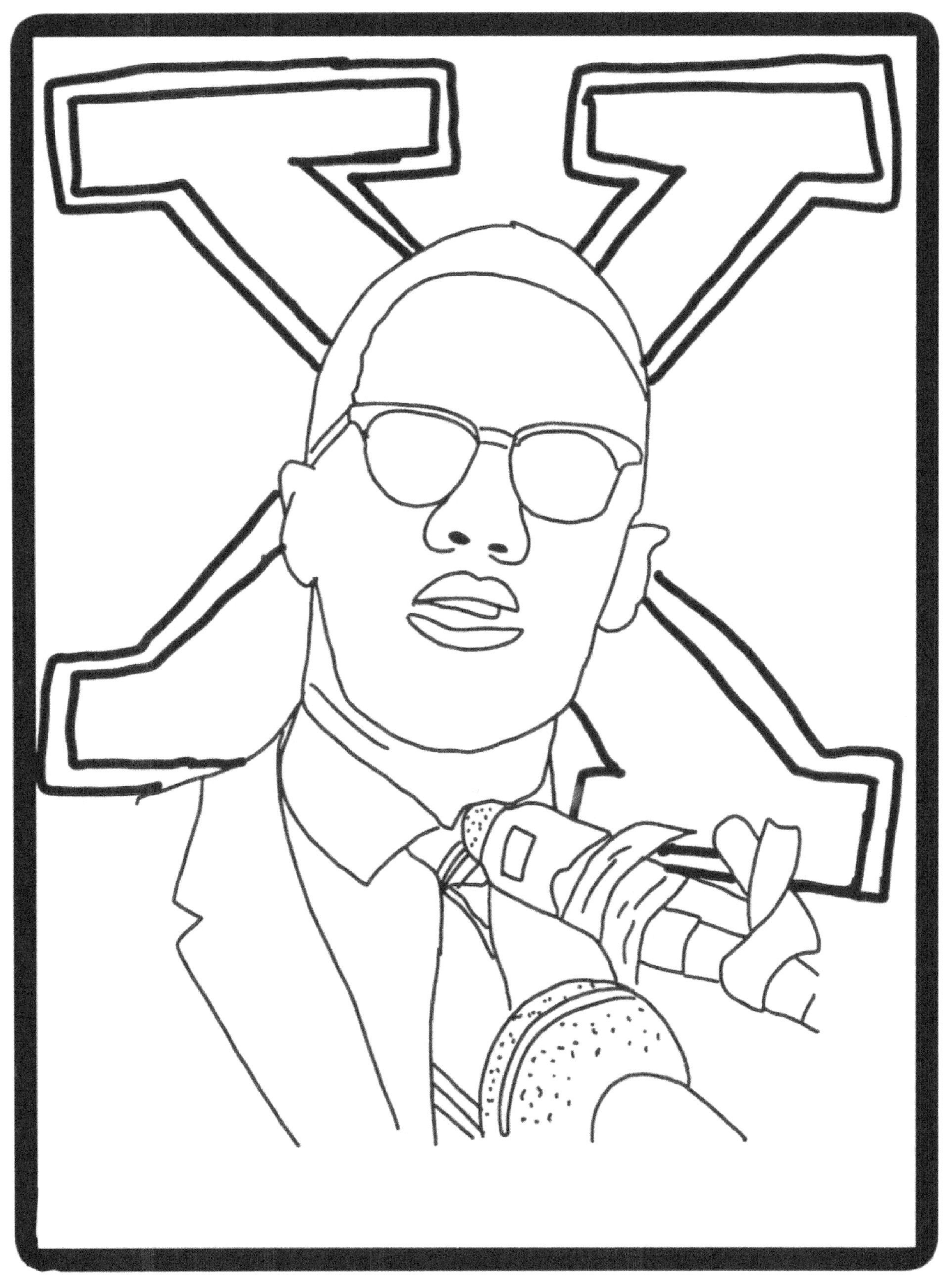

"Not everything that is faced can be changed but nothing can be changed until it is faced"

James Baldwin
Novelist-playwright-activist

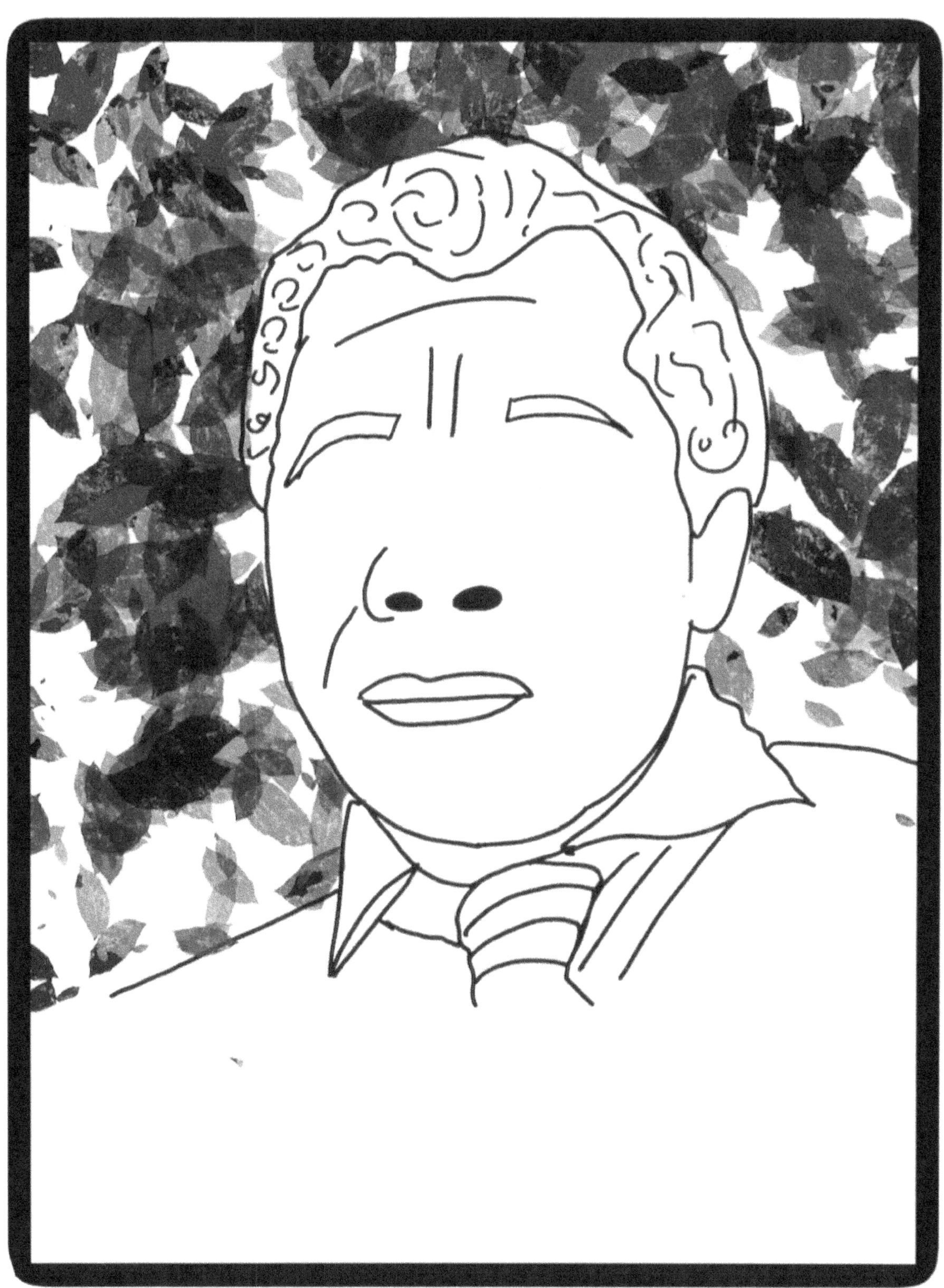

" If you see something that is not right, not fair, not just you have a moral obligation to do something about it."

John Lewis
House of Representatives Rep/Civil Rights
Activist

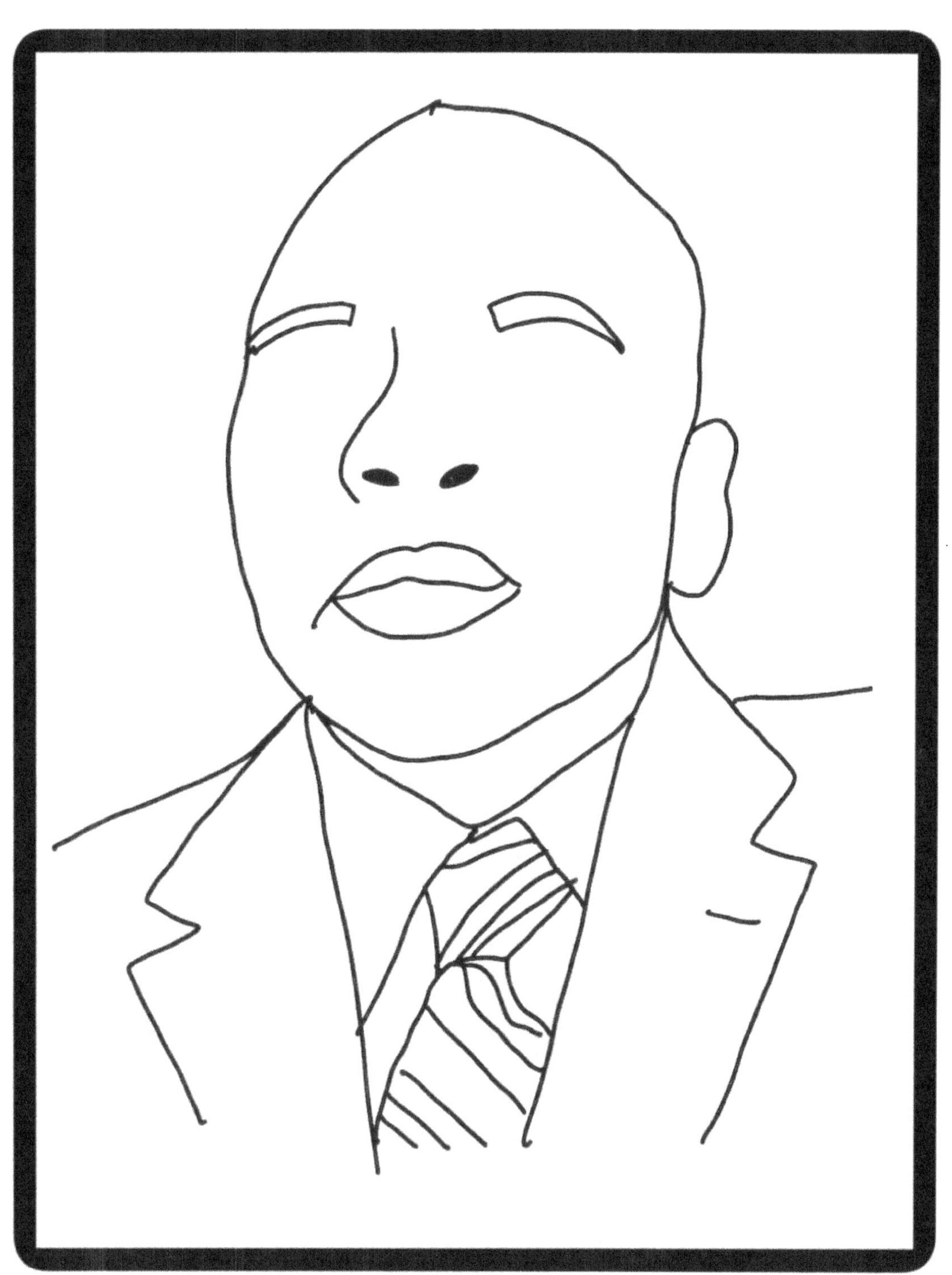

"I'll do whatever it takes to win games, whether it's sitting on a bench waving a towel, handing a cup of water to a teammate, or hitting the game-winning shot."

Kobi Bryant
NBA Player
(And so much more...R.I.P.)

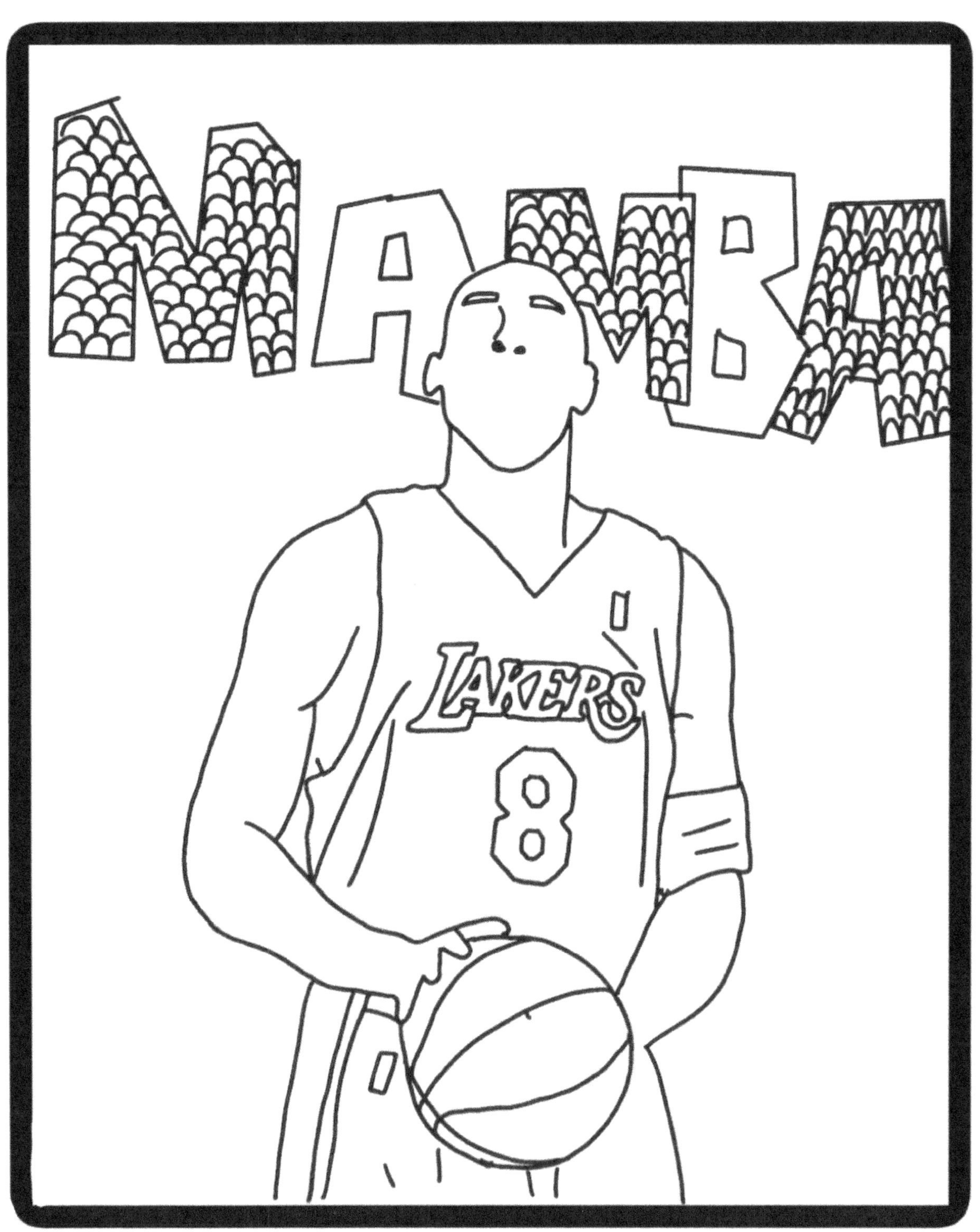

MAMBA
LAKERS
8

"The battles that count aren't the ones for gold medals. The struggles within yourself-the invisible, the inevitable battles inside all of us-that's where it's at."

Jesse Owens
Olympic Gold Medalist

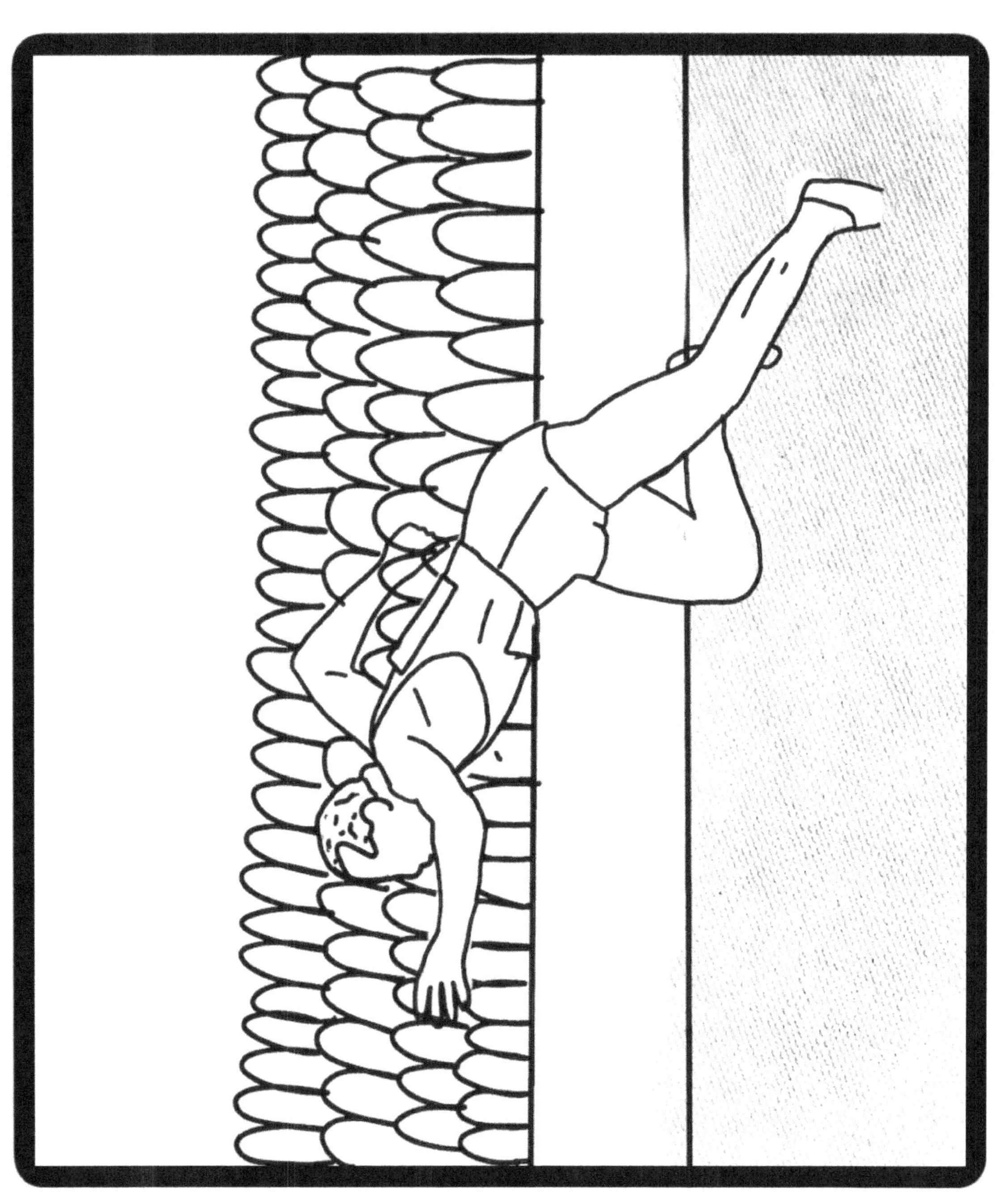

"A life is not important except in the impact it has on other lives."

Jackie Robinson
Baseball Hall of Famer
(First black man to play in the Major League Baseball)

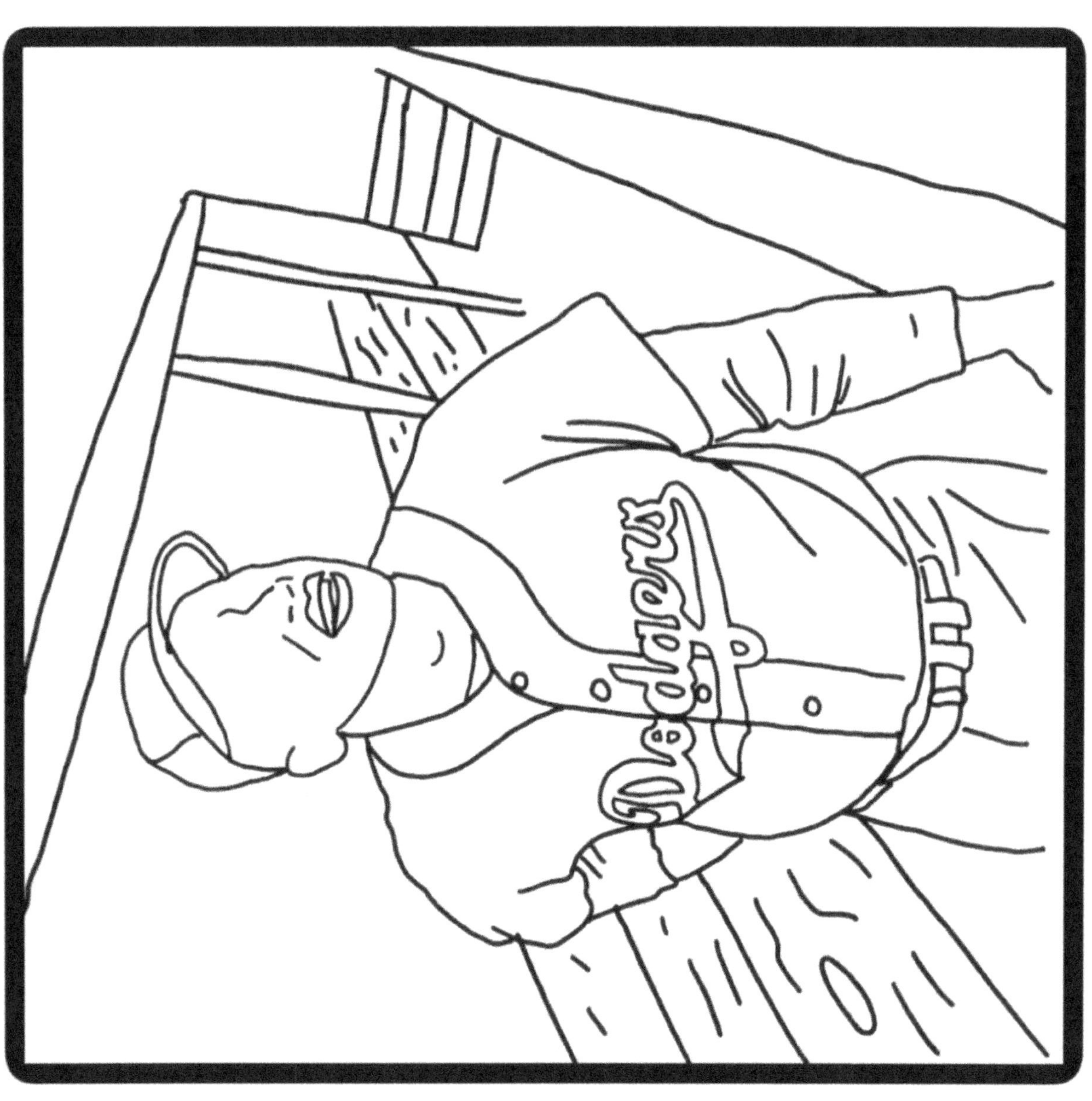
Dodgers

Creative Representation as a Movement for Change

Naomi Winston

The Black men of the world, especially in the United States, deserve a chance to be kids. They deserve the chance to grow old. Black boys deserve the chance to grow into the men that we know they can be. They deserve love, kindness, and peace.

My dad is the biggest inspiration in my life and truly demonstrates to me the unconditional effects of a father's love especially for his daughter. He has shown me how to love, how to grieve, how to succeed, and how to recover after failure.

I hope that this book helps every Black boy who uses it know the power, the love, the strength, the vulnerability, and the kindness that they have within them. I may never understand some of the experiences of the Black men in my life but I do aspire that my work can help them heal the Black boys in all of them. I hope that my work empowers Black boys not only to grow into men with a deep dedication to protecting, loving, and cherishing the people in their life but to leave space for themselves to be loved as well.

Remember, everything happens for a reason and you are everything,

Purpose of this Coloring Book:

This coloring book is more than just a few pages, words, and images. This coloring book is a reminder that you are loved, valued, and important to someone, and that someone is me. Take this coloring book and read the quotes whenever you feel down.

The empty space around some of the images was done on purpose so you can write your thoughts, your dreams, your fears, and your emotions down. I recognize that you may not be able to express yourself anywhere else in the world but know that this book is yours to be yourself in. Let your mind run free, let your creativity run free, and let your heart be open.

This books is a coloring book, a reminder, and a journal.

www.ingramcontent.com/pod-product-compliance
Lightning Source LLC
Chambersburg PA
CBHW080258030726
47593CB00009B/2533